RELIGIONS OF THE WORLD

Series Editor: Ninian Smart
Associate Editor: Richard D. Hecht

NEW
RELIGIOUS
MOVEMENTS

Elijah Siegler
College of Charleston

PEARSON
Prentice
Hall

Prentice Hall Inc., Upper Saddle River, NJ 07458

Cataloging-in-Publication Data available from the Library of Congress

Editor in Chief: Sarah Touborg
Senior Acquisitions Editor: Mical Moser
Editorial Assistant: Carla Worner
Director of Marketing: Brandy Dawson
Assistant Marketing Manager: Andrea Messineo

Pearson Education LTD.
Pearson Education Australia PTY, Limited
Pearson Education Singapore, Pte. Ltd
Pearson Education North Asia Ltd

Pearson Education, Canada, Ltd
Pearson Educación de Mexico, S.A. de C.V.
Pearson Education–Japan
Pearson Education Malaysia, Pte. Ltd

This book was designed and produced by
Laurence King Publishing Ltd., London
www.laurenceking.co.uk

Every effort has been made to contact the copyright holders, but should there be any errors or omissions,
Laurence King Publishing Ltd. would be pleased to insert the appropriate acknowledgment in any subsequent
printing of this publication.

Editor: Christine Davis
Commissioning Editor: Melanie White
Picture Researcher: Peter Kent
Designer: Andrew Shoolbred

Reviewers: D. James Atwood, Texas Christian University; Timothy Miller, University of Kansas;
Sarah M. Pike, California State University, Chico.

Picture Credits: *Cover* © CORBIS/SYGMA/Touhig Sion; *page 14* © CORBIS/Yann Arthus-Bertrand;
page 33 © CORBIS/SYGMA/Haruyoshi Yamaguchi; *page 49* Courtesy J.Z. Knight; *page 58* Private collection,
London; *page 73* © Panos Pictures/Justin Jin; *page 75* © Panos Pictures/Jeremy Horner; *page 92* © Panos
Pictures/Betty Press; *page 103* © Panos Pictures/Philippe Lissac

PEARSON
Prentice
Hall

10 9 8 7 6 5 4 3 2 1
ISBN 0–13–183478–9

Contents

Foreword

Religions of the World

The informed citizen or student needs a good overall knowledge of our small but complicated world. Fifty years ago you might have neglected religions. Now, however, we are shrewder and can see that religions and ideologies not only form civilizations but directly influence international events. These brief books provide succinct, balanced, and informative guides to the major faiths and one volume also introduces the changing religious scene as we enter the new millennium.

Today we want not only to be informed, but to be stimulated by the life and beliefs of the diverse and often complex religions of today's world. These insightful and accessible introductions allow you to explore the riches of each tradition—to understand its history, its beliefs and practices, and also to grasp its influence upon the modern world. The books have been written by a team of excellent and, on the whole, younger scholars, who represent a new generation of writers in the field of religious studies. While aware of the political and historical influences of religion, these authors aim to present the religion's spiritual side in a fresh and interesting way. So, whether you are interested simply in descriptive knowledge of a faith, or in exploring its spiritual message, you will find these introductions invaluable.

The emphasis in these books is on the modern period, because every religious tradition has transformed itself in the face of the traumatic experiences of the last two hundred years or more. Colonialism, industrialization, nationalism, revivals of religion, new religions, world wars, revolutions, and social transformations have not left faith unaffected and have drawn on religious and anti-religious forces to reshape our world. Modern technology in the last twenty-five years—from the Boeing 747 to the world wide web—has made our globe seem a much smaller place. Even the Moon's magic has been captured by technology.

We meet in these books people of the modern period as a sample of the many changes over the last few centuries. At the same time, each book provides a valuable insight into the different dimensions of the religion: its teachings, narratives, organizations, rituals, and experiences. In touching on these features, each volume gives a rounded view of the tradition, enabling you to understand what it means to belong to a particular faith. As the Native American proverb has it: "Never judge a person without walking a mile in his moccasins."

To assist you further in your exploration, a number of useful reference aids are included. Each book contains a chronology, glossary, annotated reading list, and index; where appropriate they also feature a map, pronunciation guide, and list of festivals. A selection of images provide examples of religious art, symbols, and contemporary practices. Focus boxes explore aspects of the faith in more detail.

I hope you will find these introductions enjoyable and illuminating. Brevity is supposed to be the soul of wit: it can also turn out to be what we need in the first instance in introducing cultural and spiritual themes.

Ninian Smart
Santa Barbara, 1998

Preface

Judging from the several new introductory books on New Religious Movements (NRMs) for students or general readers on the market now, it is an exciting time to be writing about or studying NRMs. These new publications will provide a needed corrective to older writings on NRMs, which typically take one of two approaches to understanding their subject. Either they assume that NRMs are a sociological problem to be solved by asking and answering a series of questions—Who would join a NRM? Do NRMs really engage in brainwashing? Why do some NRMs become violent?—or else they describe NRMs one by one in an alphabetical or chronological list.

These, I would argue, are not the most interesting and useful approaches. The sociological approach can imply that NRMs are something that has "happened" to the Western world since the 1960s, rather than a normal response to cultural and social change, which is how I see them. The encyclopedic approach can reduce NRMs to exotic curiosities.

This book takes neither approach, but instead is inspired by the phenomenological method championed by Ninian Smart, the founding editor of the Religions of the World series. For Ninian, phenomenology required informed empathy, and this is how I have tried to present the practices and values of selected New Religious Movements. As I was trained as a historian, I thought it important to include some historical background to NRMs, at least a sufficient quantity of names and dates to be of use.

This book also tries to get at some of the larger questions in the academic field of religious studies, albeit from an oblique angle. Religious identity, prejudice, globalization, and church–state relations are some of the issues touched on here just enough to provoke thought or generate discussion. I hope this book can serve as a jumping off point for students to pursue their own interests in NRMs. Books cannot replicate the intellectual satisfaction and stimulation to be gained from first-hand research into NRMs. The list of recommended readings and websites at the end of the book should help here, too.

I would like to thank my family and my editor Melanie White at Laurence King, in both cases for their infinite patience. I thank three of my teachers in Santa Barbara without whom this book could not have been written: Ninian Smart, whom knowing in the last few years of his life was a privilege and a joy; Richard Hecht, the new series editor, who has shown me such support (as he has for so many of his students), including giving me the opportunity to write this book; and J. Gordon Melton, a generous and engaging mentor whose intellectual influence should be quite obvious in these pages. I'd also like to thank colleagues in the field of religious studies who have informed this work with their knowledge and/or editorial skill: David Palmer, Zeff Bjerken, and most of all Kerry Mitchell, good friends all.

Finally, I'd like to thank the students in my New Religious Movements classes (at Wilfrid Laurier University in 2004 and at the College of Charleston in 2005) for their enthusiasm and honesty as I worked various ideas from this book into my lectures. I look forward to forcing future students into buying this book.

I would like to dedicate this book to everyone mentioned above, and indeed to all my teachers, colleagues, and students so far, three categories that wonderfully expand, shift, and overlap over the years.

Elijah Siegler
December 2005

Timeline

1830	Joseph Smith founds Latter-day Saints (Mormons) in upstate New York
1836	Anti-Catholic cult exposé *Awful Disclosures of Maria Monk* published
1838	Phineas P. Quimby begins to practice faith healing and hypnotism in Maine
	Tenrikyo founded by Nakayama Miki in Japan
1844	Joseph Smith murdered by angry mob in Illinois
	In Persia, Bab-ud-Din declares himself the Twelfth Imam, gains followers known as Babis
1847	At the end of the Great Trek, Latter-day Saints arrive in Utah
1848	First séances conducted in New York: birth of Spiritualist movement
1851	In China, Hong Xiuquan proclaims Heavenly Kingdom of Great Peace
1853	In Persia, Baha'i faith founded by Baha'u'llah
1857	Spiritism founded by Allen Kardec in France
1859	Konkokyo founded by Kawate Bunjiro in Japan
1860	Cheondogyo founded in Korea
1868	First modern American Rosicrucian group founded by Paschal Beverley Randolph
1875	Theosophical Society of America founded by H.S. Olcott and Madame Blavatsky
1879	Mary Baker Eddy founds First Church of Christ, Scientist
1888	Hermetic Order of the Golden Dawn founded in London, triggering an esoteric revival
1891	Ahmadiyya movement begins in India
	Unity School, first New Thought denomination, founded by

	Myrtle and Charles Fillmore in Kansas City
1893	The World's Parliament of Religions in Chicago brings Asian religious teachers to the U.S.
1894	After attending the Parliament of Religions, Swami Vivekenanda establishes Vedanta Society
1910	Hazrat Inayat Khan settles in the West and founds the Sufi Order
1911	The Zulu Isaiah Shembe founds the Nazareth Baptist Church in South Africa. It will become one of the largest African Initated Churches
1917	True Jesus Church founded in Beijing
1920	Swami Yogananda arrives in the United States. He will incorporate the Self-Realization Fellowship fifteen years later
1921	Simon Kimbangu begins healing mission in the Congo, which later grows to be the largest African Initiated Church
1926	Ngo Van Chieu founds Cao Dai religion in Vietnam
1928	Hassan al Banna founds Muslim Brotherhood in Egypt
1930s	Yiguandao and other syncretic millennial groups founded in China
1930	W.D. Fard begins teaching in Detroit, laying foundation for the Nation of Islam
1937	Soka Gakkai founded in Japan
1938	Publication of *The Chaos of the Cults* by Jan Van Baalen, first book of the modern Christian countercult movement
1950s	Birth of qigong in China
1953	Jean Rouch's documentary *Les Maîtres Fous* ("The Mad Masters"), about a possession cult in Ghana, brings attention to African neo-traditional NRMs

1954	Gerald Gardner publishes *Witchcraft Today*, inspiring the growth of Wiccan religion
	Sun Myung Moon founds Unification Church in South Korea
	L. Ron Hubbard founds Church of Scientology in Los Angeles
1955	Gesehe Wangyal, a Mongolian Master of Tibetan Buddhism, arrives in the United States. Three years later he will open the first Tibetan monastery in the U.S.
1956	Aetherius Society, a UFO group, founded by George King in the U.K.
1959	Maharishi Mahesh Yogi introduces Transcendental Meditation to the U.S.
1963	Jane Roberts channels Seth, ushering in modern age of channeling
1965	New Immigration Act passed by U.S. ends racist quota system
	Eckankar founded by Paul Twitchell in California
	Swami Prabhupada brings International Society for Krishna Consciousness to the West
1969	Sikh guru Yogi Bhajan founds the Healthy, Happy, Holy Organization (3HO), which later changes its name to Sikh Dharma
1970	Buddhist teacher Chogyam Trungpa arrives in the U.S.; founds Naropa Institute four years later
1971	Guru Maharaj Ji arrives in U.S. from India as head of Divine Light Mission
	The Pagan Federation, an international informational and support network, is founded in the U.K.
1972	FREECOG founded as first organized anticult movement. Two years later it changes name to Citizens Freedom Foundation
1973	In France, Claude Vorhillon's encounter with extraterrestrial beings leads him to found the

	Raelian Movement, the world's largest UFO religion
1974	Jach Pursel begins channeling Lazaris
1977	J.Z. Knight begins channeling Ramtha
1978	People's Temple massacre in Jonestown, Guyana; 918 dead
1979	The U.S. senate begins hearings on "the cult phenomenon"
1981	Bhagwan Shree Rajneesh leaves India and opens his commune in Oregon
Late 1980s	"Qigong fever" peaks in China, as charismatic masters attract millions of followers
1989	Osama bin Laden founds Al-Qaeda
1992	Falun gong founded by Li Hongzhi in northeastern China
1993	During stand-off with law enforcement, Branch Davidian compound in Waco, Texas, is set aflame. Eighty people dead.
1994	Fifty-three members of Order of Solar Temple kill themselves in France, Switzerland, and Quebec. Sixteen more commit suicide in 1995 and five more in 1997
1995	Aum Shinrikyo releases deadly sarin gas in the Tokyo subway, killing twelve and poisoning thousands
1996	The Cult Awareness Network is sued and bankrupted; its name and logo are bought by members of the Church of Scientology
1997	Thirty-nine members of UFO group Heaven's Gate commit suicide near San Diego, California
1999	Falun gong banned by Chinese government; members persecuted
2000	780 members of the Movement for the Restoration of the Ten Commandments, a Marian apparition group, commit suicide or are murdered in Uganda
	France passes strictest "anticult" law in Western Europe
2004	Shoko Asahara, leader of Aum Shinrikyo, sentenced to death

Glastonbury, U.K., April 30—It is the eve of Beltane, a holiday that celebrates fertility and the coming of summer, and one of eight festivals that make up the "wheel of the year" for **Neopagans**. This town in the southwest of England has fewer than ten thousand permanent residents, but its small size is belied by its importance as a center of new religious activity. At any time of year, but particularly at important holidays such as this one, Glastonbury serves as a pilgrimage site for people from around the world. Pagans come to Glastonbury because they believe it was once the center of Celtic spirituality, a dominant tradition of pre-Christian Europe, which, driven underground for centuries, has now been revived.

Glastonbury is a place to learn a variety of spiritual techniques, from aromatherapy (using fragrances to relieve stress and cure illness) to reiki (projecting energy through massage). The town is also home to several specific religious groups, some based here since the 1960s, which might be termed New Religious Movements. The High Street (main shopping street) of Glastonbury is crowded with tourists buying handmade artwork, perhaps depicting King Arthur and his Knights, alluding to the belief that Glastonbury is the site of Avalon, the legendary land described in the tales of the Knights of the Round Table.

As evening descends, hundreds of Neopagans of all varieties, from all parts of the U.K. and elsewhere—some dressed in T-shirts and carrying backpacks, others in white robes and holding staffs—make their way up to Glastonbury Tor, a hill on the edge of town, which is crowned by a tower. The Tor, like the Stonehenge stone circle nearby, has become a center of ritual activity because of its connection to ancient ceremonies and the particularly strong spiritual energies that are said to be experienced there. Participants in the all-night Beltane celebration may make bonfires or form drumming circles. Soon after sunrise, various local groups—such as the Druid College of Avalon, which sees itself as the restoration of a **Druidic** university—will perform rituals to welcome the day, including making an offering to the spirits of the four directions.

Tokyo, Japan, February 27, 2004—In a packed courtroom, an eight-year-long trial is coming to an end. Shoko Asahara, a longhaired and bearded forty-eight-year-old former yoga instructor, is found guilty of all charges and is sentenced to death. As the leader of the New Religious Movement known as Aum Shinrikyo, he has been judged responsible for the deaths of twenty-seven people and the injuring of thousands. As the district court judge reads the sentence out loud, Asahara seems to not understand, grimacing and moaning at random but not uttering a word. He has remained silent in court for several years. Is he insane? Has he achieved transcendence, the stated goal of the religion he founded? Or is this a final cynical, heartless ploy to avoid taking responsibility for his actions?

Asahara is the last of twelve Aum Shinrikyo members to be sentenced to death by hanging, a punishment rarely invoked in Japan. The mass arrests and trials were brought on by Aum releasing sarin, a poison nerve gas, into the Tokyo subway during rush hour in March 1995.

That year, Aum Shinrikyo was a legally registered religion with approximately one thousand members living in communal homes, while another ten thousand supported the movement but kept their "outside" jobs and family. Aum Shinrikyo, founded in 1984, emphasized ascetic practices to attain psychic ability and spiritual enlightenment, and owed much to Asahara's study of Tibetan **Buddhism**. The growing movement's initial optimistic doctrine of universal salvation was replaced by an apocalypticism and culture of coercive violence, which culminated in the Tokyo subway killings. Aum saw these as a preemptive attack on a society that was about to shut them down.

At the time of Asahara's sentencing the movement still had over one thousand members, but in renaming itself **Aleph**, formally apologizing for the violence, and offering restitution to the victims, the group hoped to distance themselves from their former leader. Nonetheless, the group was kept under government surveillance and its activities severely limited. Asahara's trial was one of the most important and expensive in Japanese history and changed the way new religions are thought of in Japan.

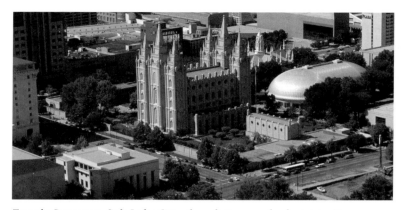

Temple Square in Salt Lake City, the religious and administrative center of the Church of Jesus Christ of Latter-day Saints. Behind the spired Temple is the dome of the Mormon Tabernacle.

Salt Lake City, U.S.A.—On this Sunday morning, like most others in this capital city of the state of Utah, the **Mormon** Tabernacle Choir is performing at the Mormon Tabernacle in Temple Square. At precisely 9.30 a.m., 325 men and women dressed in red robes take the stage and begin singing a mix of Christian hymns and patriotic American tunes for an audience of visitors and locals. All those taking part in what President Ronald Reagan called "America's choir" are volunteers, and members in good standing of the **Church of Jesus Christ of Latter-day Saints (LDS)**. Indeed, it is expected that all LDS members will regularly volunteer their time and money to various Church activities, whether administrative, missionary, or cultural, while at the same time maintaining successful careers and stable families.

The choir's concerts have been broadcast weekly over the CBS radio network since 1929, thereby making them the country's longest running radio feature. The home of the choir dates from 1867, but before that Mormon pioneers used a bowery (a canopy of trees) for their tabernacle. The current tabernacle also hosts the semiannual LDS church conferences as well as major Salt Lake civic events. Other tabernacles perform the same function in the smaller Mormon towns of Bountiful and Logan.

Salt Lake City Tabernacle itself is a large building that sits on Temple Square in the center of town, its impressive dome contrasting with the graceful spires of the nearby LDS Temple, a building used for important rituals and closed to all non-Mormons. Also on the pleasant square are public gardens, LDS administration buildings, and the LDS Visitors' Center, where neatly dressed young women (in fact, Mormon missionaries) will guide tourists through dioramas depicting the dramatic history of this new American religion—from its 1830 founding in upstate New York to the persecution of its original followers as they moved across the country, their 1847 arrival in the Utah territory, and their subsequent worldwide missionary activities.

These three sketches present current activities of three very different New Religious Movements (NRMs) on three continents. Neopagans, Aum Shinrikyo, and the Latter-day Saints have little in common politically, doctrinally, or ritually. Their geography, history, and demographics are wildly disparate. These scenarios represent but three out of the thousands of New Religious Movements in the world today. Does this demonstrate the disparity and variety of NRMs or the meaninglessness of the term itself?

Of course, these three groups share a few characteristics in common. First, they are all fairly new. Aum Shinrikyo is twenty years old and most Neopagan groups in the U.K. are no more than thirty or forty years old. The Latter-day Saints are less than two hundred years old. (Yet even these assertions are problematic: the three groups see themselves as modern expressions of ancient religions, as do many other NRMs. Neopagans believe they are continuing the spirituality of pre-Christian Europe, while Aum Shinrikyo sees itself as practicing an age-old form of Buddhism. The Latter-day Saints assert they have restored the original Christian Church.)

Second, all three groups are religious. This seems fairly incontrovertible no matter what definition of religion is used. They all deal with supernatural or unseen beings and they all provide an internally coherent series of answers to the ultimate questions.

Third, they all exist in tension with society to one degree or another. While Neopagans are generally tolerated and some of their ideas may even seem mainstream in parts of Europe, many of them report feeling socially marginalized and being discriminated against or even verbally and physically attacked. Aum Shinrikyo was regarded as unorthodox before the crimes committed by its members came to light; thereafter it was known as the "Doomsday Cult" and widely despised throughout Japan. In the first half-century of their existence, the Latter-day Saints were probably subject to more legal and physical attacks by the U.S. government, as well as more popular prejudice, than any NRM before or since. The hundred years since then have seen a steady climb towards the mainstream, even as anti-Mormon hostility continues in many countries and among some segments of the American population. Are NRMs in tension with society because they pose a threat? Or are they just victims of negative stereotypes?

Stereotyping NRMs

If defining a "New Religious Movement" seems difficult, it is not because nobody knows what an NRM is but because everyone thinks they do. If you were to ask a random sampling of people to define a New Religious Movement, you would probably come up with a fairly consistent definition of NRMs as dangerous and antisocial because they brainwash unsuspecting, often lonely people into living in isolation from their friends and families, and adopting strange beliefs and rituals, while giving away their money and freedom to a charismatic leader. NRMs might also be characterized as promoting abnormal sexuality (which could be anything from celibacy to group marriage) and being often involved in violent acts. These commonly held ideas about NRMs have been shaped by the media. TV and newspaper reports about NRMs rarely focus on their neighborly qualities or charitable activities. Instead, NRMs are noticed only when they are violent or deceitful.

By now, many readers will be thinking that the term "NRM" is just a polite word for "cult," which is what the media (and some scholars) typically calls New Religious Movements. And indeed, the term preferred in this book, "New Religious Movement," was adopted by scholars in recent years precisely because the word "cult" had acquired such unabashedly pejorative connotations. (How the descriptive term "cult" became associated with evil religious activity will be discussed in Chapter 2.)

While other terms have been suggested, most notably "alternative" and "fringe" religions, "New Religious Movements" has become the scholarly standard. The term was translated from the Japanese term *shin shukyo*, used to describe the plethora of new movements arising in post-war Japan (see Chapter 5). Ironically, the word "cult" with all its negative connotations has been recently transliterated to become the Japanese term *karuto*, coined mainly to describe Aum Shinrikyo and certain Western religious imports.

Whatever they are called, New Religious Movements are defined by outsiders, not practitioners. There are billions of people around the world who would proclaim, "I am a Christian" and millions who would announce, "I am a Jew," but very few who would state, "I am a member of an NRM" (and fewer still who would say, "I belong to a cult"!). The very concept of an NRM or cult has been defined in the West by outside, often hostile interests including conservative Christians, the mass media, some scholars, and the professional anticult movement. Chapter 2 will examine this definitional process in more detail.

Defining NRMs

Whatever the problems inherent in defining NRMs, a working definition is needed, if only to justify what gets included and excluded. What makes an NRM "new"? The earliest groups under consideration here were founded in the second quarter of the nineteenth century. The date is more than arbitrary: this period saw an explosion of data about "world religions," which sparked the development of the comparative and "scientific" study of religion. It also witnessed the rise of mass communication, creating an appetite for what is now called "tabloid journalism," which focuses on the bizarre and scandalous. Both these processes contributed to the conceptualization of a "new religious movement." Therefore, the earliest NRM considered in this text is the Mormon Church (the Latter-day Saints).

What makes an NRM "religious"? A standard definition of religion is a system that posits the existence of supernatural or transhuman beings and proposes answers to the ultimate questions of life. Thus, therapeutic and political movements will not be discussed in this book. This is often a difficult distinction to make. Many **New Age** groups, for example, are based around the teaching of a specific therapeutic technique such as massage or dietary restrictions. Many far-right political groups, including some survivalists and neo-Nazis, have a quasi-Christian focus. But these groups will not be discussed in this book.

Given the above, what makes an NRM different from any other religious group that might have arisen in the last two hundred years (say, the Southern Baptist Convention or Reform Judaism)? The answer, in three words, is tension with society. NRMs, by definition, exist in latent or overt tension with the larger social world they inhabit. According to the scholar of new religious movements J. Gordon Melton, the religious organizations in any country can be divided into the following categories:

1. Churches or established religions (which have "the power to designate the boundaries of acceptable deviation in belief and practice and identify those groups that fall outside those boundaries.")
2. Ethnic religions, the religion of particular linguistic, cultural, or racial minorities (which are generally seen as acceptable by the established religions "as long as they continue to limit their activity to their own ethnic constituency.")
3. Sects or denominations (smaller groups within the larger established religion but "differing in that they are perceived as more strict on matters of belief, more diligent in practice, and more fervent in worship.")
4. NRMs—comprising everything that is left over. Thus Melton defines NRMs as "those religious groups that have been found, from the perspective of the dominant religious community ... not just different, but unacceptably different. At the same time, the list of groups that would be considered under the rubric of "new religions" would differ from country to country and always be under negotiation."[1]

As Melton stresses, context is everything: in the United States, the United Methodist Church is one of the largest, most mainstream religious organizations. In Greece, where the government keeps tabs on all non-Orthodox Christian religions, the United Methodists are labeled a dangerous cult. In India, **Hinduism** is the dominant religion. In countries with a substantial South Asian minority, such as Fiji, Hinduism is counted as an ethnic religion. In many countries of Western Europe, Hinduism manifests itself as a group of often unwelcome NRMs.

By now, the reader may be asking impatiently: Well, what do NRMs actually believe in and practice to make them so bad? In fact, NRMs have no shared characteristics except their extreme diversity. Melton has argued that in terms of belief and practice, NRMs resemble the religious tradition from which they derive (sometimes called their "parent group") more than each other. For example, the **Hare Krishnas**, the **Family** (formerly the Children of God), and the Church of **Scientology** are all generally considered NRMs. Other than their tension with society, they have little in common. The Krishnas are more like other Hindu groups than they are like other NRMs, and the Family comes out of the **Jesus People** movements. Scientology, although an extremely eclectic movement, belongs to the Western **esoteric** tradition as will be described in Chapter 3.

Explaining NRMs

Why are there so many NRMs? This question will occur to anyone who studies NRMs, even briefly. The question is somewhat misleading, however, because it rests on two possible, yet mutually exclusive, suppositions. The first assumes there are more NRMs now than in the past. The second assumes the rate of appearance of NRMs (even if they are not called that) has always been high. In other words the first supposition sees NRMs as an expression of change, the second as a demonstration of continuity. We will cover both suppositions in turn.

Social change

The academic study of New Religious Movements has been conceptualized, for the most part, by sociologists of religion. Sociology is, of course, less interested in specific historic or cultural contexts than in larger social processes, and one of the major processes is known as "secularization." The secularization thesis (here using the terminology of the preeminent sociologist of religion, Peter Berger) states that with the onset of modernity, religion, which formerly gave society an overarching structure, is forced to contend with the forces of pluralism (whereby many faiths compete in a given society) and privatization (whereby faith can only be expressed individually and voluntarily).[2] Thus the tendency is for society to become more secular over time; some sociologists have even predicted that religion, stripped of its status, will in due course wither away. The presence of NRMs, it might seem, would disprove the secularization thesis by demonstrating the continued vitality of religion. But certain sociologists hold that NRMs have arisen precisely as a response to secularization, modernity, and the decline of traditional religions. NRMs represent the "last gasp of religion," a retrenchment of anti-modern faith in the face of pluralized and privatized modernity. However, the secularization thesis has lost some of its academic currency in recent years, as it has become increasingly obvious that, outside of the European state churches, religions are flourishing, not withering, and that most societies are becoming less secular, not more.

The sociologists of religion Rodney Stark and William Bainbridge have advanced a more nuanced version of the secularization thesis.[3] For them, NRMs arise cyclically, in response to the periodic collapse of dominant religions that occurs when these religions fail to provide the "compensators" (to use Stark's term) that people expect, including solace for the bereaved, answers for the perplexed, and community for the lonely. NRMs function, for Stark and Bainbridge, like new, improved brands of consumer products, trying to get some market share. Another eminent sociologist, Charles Y. Glock, argued that people join NRMs because of present or anticipated deprivation of various sorts, including economic deprivation, social deprivation (the lack of religious communities or extended families), or psychic deprivation (feelings of fragmentation or alienation).[4]

Robert Bellah, a sociologist of religion studying NRMs in the San Francisco Bay Area in the early 1970s, argued that new religions were "successor movements" to the movements of political protest and cultural experimentation that flourished among the youth of the 1960s.[5] Societal upheavals such as political assassinations, race riots, the war in Southeast Asia, and the Watergate scandal turned young people, so his theory goes, off politics and into the arms of waiting "cults."

These sociological explanations for NRMs—as the last retrenchment of religion in a secular society, as an upstart brand name filling a market niche in the religious economy, as a personal bulwark against feelings of deprivation, or as the successor to failed political protest—each have some truth to them, and, as their respective originators would be the first to admit, should be considered as neither comprehensive nor mutually exclusive. Still, they are fundamentally reductive in character, that is, they reduce the meaning of an NRM into a single, explanatory factor. These theories also characterize NRMs as reactive and passive inasmuch as they see people drawn to NRMs because of external social factors, not because of any inherently attractive or worthy characteristics of the NRMs themselves.

Historical continuity and cultural context

If historians often criticize sociologists for lacking a long-term view, this criticism applies doubly to sociologists who study NRMs. From the sociological perspective, a number of strange religions appeared suddenly in North America and Western Europe in the 1960s and 1970s and seduced the young and naive into leaving their comfortable lives. To explain why that generation was susceptible to join NRMs became the primary task of much NRM scholarship. This book, by contrast, will not spend much time asking who joins NRMs and why. We assume that people join NRMs (and other religions) for all sorts of psychological, theological, or cultural reasons. This book concentrates on putting NRMs into historical and global context and does not consider them a sociological problem.

The presence of NRMs in the West today can be explained in part by historical processes. Three of these processes are explained in the first half of the book. The West has long castigated and persecuted religions perceived to be unacceptably different, and Chapter 2 will look at the contemporary cult scare and anticult movement in that historical light. Esotericism has been an ever-present tradition running counter to mainstream religious and philosophical beliefs in the West; Chapter 3 will look at a number of NRMs as instances of revival of that often-underground tradition. The West and Asia have been engaged in a fruitful but often misunderstood religious and cultural exchange for hundreds of years; in Chapter 4, another set of NRMs are analyzed using the background of this ongoing East–West encounter.

If the first part of this book is concerned with different ways of looking at NRMs in the West, the second part takes as its guiding principle the assertion that NRMs are a global phenomenon. NRMs in the Western world represent a small percentage of NRMs worldwide: there are approximately two thousand NRMs active in the West, but overall NRMs may number in the tens of thousands. It is easy to see, then, that NRMs are not primarily a Western phenomenon but are globally distributed.

Scholars of new religions outside the modern West have been working in disciplines that have not, until recently, been in contact with each other. For example, Chinese NRMs have been studied (not always under that name) by social or popular historians of China. The fact that hundreds if not thousands of NRMs have arisen in Africa has been remarked on mainly by scholars (often with missionary backgrounds) of African Christianity. Islamic-based NRMs have been the purview of Islamicists. Similar points could be made about NRMs in Latin America, the South Pacific, and so forth.

As the academic study of NRMs has become an increasingly international discipline, it has now become possible for even a short introductory book such as this, written by and for the non-specialist, to incorporate findings from around the world. Thus Chapter 5 focuses on NRMs in East Asia; Chapter 6 looks at the NRMs of Africa and the African Diaspora; and Chapter 7 examines NRMs derived from Islam. Obviously, this selection leaves out large parts of the world—to give equal time to all NRMs everywhere would require a book many times this length. These chapters cover material that seems to be particularly overlooked or misunderstood and that has particular relevance to current events.

Studying NRMs

Why should people study New Religious Movements at all? One reason often given is that the Western world is in the throes of a "cult invasion" and that increasing millions of Americans and Europeans are members of one NRM or another. But this is far from the case. In the United States during the 1970s, when fears of the "growing cult menace" were running high, the total number of active NRM members (excluding, in this case, Mormons and other nineteenth-century Christian movements) was probably in the range of 150,000 to 300,000. Today a miniscule percentage of the population of any given country belongs to an NRM (exceptions may be, as we will see, in Japan and in some parts of Africa), and that percentage remains fairly constant. So if NRMs are not statistically significant, then why should we learn about them?

For one, the study of NRMs offers an opportunity to observe religion at its earliest stages, to watch a religious drama unfold in real-time—its formation, routinization, internal division, and so forth (everything that in older, larger religions has taken hundreds of years). In defense of New Religious Movements, a comparison with early Christianity is very often made (Buddhism and Islam also make apt comparisons with NRMs). In the first century, Christianity existed in high tension with the Roman government and with the Jewish religious establishment. Jesus was a charismatic leader, with radical ideas, including the belief in the imminent destruction of the old world and coming of a new one. This idea, known as **millennialism**, is common to many NRMs all over the world. How did this "dangerous cult" become the largest religion in the world? It is impossible to witness the birth and early growth of Christianity first hand. Although it is doubtful that any NRM will become the next Christianity, studying NRMs can give us the next best thing to observing the birth and growth of a major religion.

Another reason to study NRMs is that they often serve as laboratories of social and cultural experimentation, putting into practice society's most radical ideas. In the 1870s and 1880s, an NRM called **Theosophy** introduced Asian words like "karma" and "chakra" into the West, where today they form part of everyday vocabulary. Western NRMs were also the first to engage in communal living, multiple marriage, and eugenics (in this case pairing off couples with a mind to the genetic superiority of their offspring). Certain ideas have never been adapted into mainstream society, however. For example, polygamy, the practice of taking multiple wives, which the LDS (Mormons) saw as divinely mandated, caused the Mormon Church to be reviled by its non-Mormon neighbors and persecuted by the U.S. government. Indeed the 1890 doctrine that reversed Mormon policy on polygamy is widely seen as a concession to the Federal government.

On the other hand, sometimes NRMs are harbingers of overall social change. Around the same time as the Mormon Church was practicing polygamy, many other NRMs had women as their spiritual and temporal leaders, including the **Adventist** movement, led by Ellen G. White; **Christian Science**, initiated and overseen by Mary Baker Eddy; and the Theosophical movement directed by a series of powerful women, beginning with its co-founder, Madame Blavatsky. In the late nineteenth century, the practice of women serving as church leaders seemed as bizarre as polygamy. Today, women are in positions of authority in virtually all mainstream religious (and non-religious) organizations. Indeed, this is in large part thanks to the organized feminist movement, which shared many of its members with another nineteenth-century NRM, **Spiritualism**.

Another reason why NRMs reward careful study is their small size and fixed boundaries, which offer us a good opportunity to examine important social processes in miniature, including prejudice, religious revivalism, cultural exchanges, and the causes and effects of modernization and globalization. All these processes will be described in the following chapters. Finally, NRMs are inherently interesting. This is just this author's opinion, but perhaps the reader will share it by the end of the book.

NRMs as Modern Heresy | 2

There is an episode in the ninth season of the half-hour animated sit-com "The Simpsons," in which Homer joins the Movementarians, a dubious new religion that promises "a new and better life ... on our distant home planet, Blisstonia."[1] After endlessly chanting in praise of the founder to the tune of the old "Batman" TV theme song  ("na-na-na-na-Leader!"), Homer (and most of the rest of the town of Springfield) is convinced that the religion's Leader will lead them away on his spaceship.

Homer gives the Movementarians his life savings, the Simpsons' house, and "a commitment to ten trillion years of labor," and moves his family to the cult's compound, where members must participate in a mass marriage ceremony and work at subsistence agriculture while the Leader rides by in a Rolls-Royce, covering them (if they are lucky) in road dust. Although members are "free to leave" the compound, escape is all but impossible as it involves maneuvering through a wasteland of land mines and barbed wire. Eventually it is revealed that the Leader's spaceship is made of paper and that its whirring sound comes from him blowing air through a comb. The Leader tries unsuccessfully to flee, weighted down with bags of his followers' money.

This episode provokes laughs of recognition because it exaggerates our popular stereotypes of "cults": the Movementarians use deceptive recruiting practices, and isolate members from the rest of society while forcing them to live in poverty. Like many "cult" leaders, the Leader is a charlatan out for cash. The episode also contains numerous jokes directed at specific NRMs—including Rajneesh, Scientology, and the **Moonies**.

Where do these instantly recognizable "cult" stereotypes come from? This chapter traces the history not of NRMs but of how and why the prejudices against them developed. We will see how the modern cult stereotype is a cultural construction with a certain internal logic to its representation.

A Short History of Heresy

Categorizing rival religious beliefs and practices as "strange," "destructive," or "deceptive" predates the modern cult stereotype by nearly two thousand years, and may have little to do with the actual negative qualities of the rival religion. As NRM scholar James Lewis put it: "The labeling and persecution of minorities is usually more of a response to doubts and anxieties about norms and values within the dominant culture than a response to tangible threats from minority groups."[2] From a sociological perspective, one of religion's primary functions is to create and maintain both personal and group identity. Our religion gives us a sense of who we are and who is like us. Religion can also strengthen identity in a negative way: those who do not worship the same god we worship or belong to the same church we belong to are *not* like us.

Using religion as a boundary marker seems to be a natural human characteristic, found in practically all cultures. As the theorist of religion Jonathan Z. Smith states, "the most common form of classifying religions ... is dualistic and can be reduced, regardless of what differentium is employed, to "theirs" and "ours."[3] One indication of the persistent power of the "theirs" category of religion is how often the most common names for religious adherents began as epithets created by outsiders. To call someone a **Quaker**, a Mormon, or even a Protestant was originally an insult, directed towards the religious "other."

The concept of **heresy** is most important to understand this process of defining religions as "other" in order to strengthen your own religious identity. A heresy is a false belief, in other words a belief that contradicts those of the group that is defining the heresy. The word comes from the Greek *haresis*, which means a group of people having a clear doctrinal identity (with no value judgment implied). Early Christian writers used the term to refer to the teaching of false doctrine, deviant from orthodox Christianity. Like the word "cult," the word "heretic" is not used as a self-identification. "Heretics" do not see themselves as having false beliefs but rather as preserving or restoring a religious truth.

Although the word heresy comes out of the Christian tradition, most religions also define rivals in terms of "false doctrine." Next to Christianity, Islam is probably the religion most concerned with heresy. There are several words in Arabic that have similar connotations to the English word "heresy." *Bid'a*, for example, means a doctrine or practice not known in the time of Muhammad; but the Arabic word most often translated as "heretic" is *kafir*, which means "unbeliever."

Other traditions that have produced strong arguments directed against heretics include rabbinic Judaism (which has its own term for heresy: *minim*) and **neo-Confucianism**. **Daoism**, often misinterpreted as an all-embracing philosophy that would have no concern with enforcing orthodox belief, in fact has been preoccupied with heresy since its early days. One of the earliest texts of religious Daoism (from the second century C.E.) included several precepts charging the reader with avoiding non-orthodox texts and false methods. Early Daoist writers seemed particularly outraged with self-proclaimed Daoist teachers who practiced "false arts" under the guise of the "teachings of the Dao."[4]

But it is the Christian concept of heresy that is the direct precursor of the modern cult stereotype. The early Christian world was wracked with theological disputes, including those over the nature of the body of Christ. The mainstream Christian position, that Christ was at once fully human and fully divine, was in part adopted to distance the dominant Church from the beliefs of other early Christian groups, which were later labeled heresies. For example, Arianism held that Jesus, as Son, was subordinate to God, the Father, whereas Docetism maintained that Jesus' human body was an illusion. Other early heresies more closely resembled the modern day "cult" stereotype, such as Montanism, which was led by charismatic leaders who used trances to prophesy the end of the world. The most widely condemned heresy of the ancient world was Gnosticism, which offered a complete alternative reading of Christianity and will be discussed in the next chapter. Some scholars argue that mainstream Christian theology developed largely as a reaction against these heretical movements. In other words, heresy precedes orthodoxy and gives rise to it.

The next notable period for Christian heretics and their persecutors was from the twelfth to the sixteenth centuries. As the medieval Church was defining itself politically and geographically and consolidating its identity, groups such as the Waldensians, the Cathars, and the Hussites were persecuted for their unorthodox beliefs. Significantly, the Church did not punish these groups itself but hunted them down and turned them over to secular governments for execution. In other words, like New Religious Movements today, medieval heresies were socially as well as religiously deviant.

Christian heresy after the Reformation

From a Catholic perspective, the Protestant Reformation might be seen as simply the latest and most successful of the medieval heresies. Beginning in the sixteenth century, Protestantism rejected the authority of the Catholic Church, and spread ideas about freedom of conscience and individual interpretation of Scripture, so that numerous autonomous churches flourished. But Protestants themselves were not shy about persecuting other Protestants as heretics.

One group often persecuted by fellow Protestants as well as the Catholic Church was the **Anabaptists**, named for their practice of "re-baptizing" adult believers. Sometimes referred to as the "left" or "radical" wing of the Reformation, the Anabaptists practiced communal living, rejected all secular and religious authority, and had a millennialist worldview. Founded in 1525, Anabaptism quickly became one of the most feared and hated "cults" in Europe, and many Anabaptists were executed for the crime of practicing adult baptism.

Persecuted throughout Europe for their pacifist and communitarian beliefs, many Anabaptist groups found refuge in America, where today their descendants, including the Amish, the Mennonites, and the Hutterites, are known for their simple, pastoral way of life. Many Amish continue to travel in horse-drawn buggies, for example. Although Anabaptism is still known as an alternative religion, present-day adherents live peacefully alongside mainstream society and are not thought of as members of a cult. Today, of course, many Christian denominations practice adult baptism.

Other radical Protestant sects came to America from the seventeenth century onwards, fleeing persecution. The **Puritans** and the Quakers both sought to purge the Church of England of what they considered to be unacceptable traces of Roman Catholicism; the Church of England in turn saw both groups as unacceptably different. Pacifists like the Anabaptists, the Quakers (known formally as the Society of Friends) settled in the American colony of Pennsylvania where they quickly formed their own mainstream establishments. The Puritans were subject to particularly brutal punishment by the English authorities. For example, in 1630 a Puritan man was sentenced to life imprisonment, had his property confiscated, his nose slit, an ear cut off, and his forehead branded "S.S." (sower of sedition).

Puritans emigrated to the New England colonies, where they themselves severely punished religious dissent. One dissenter was the Baptist Roger Williams, who was eventually expelled from the Massachusetts Bay colony and founded the colony of Rhode Island. The Puritans, like the early Christian leaders and the medieval Church, seemed to fear religious difference because they saw it as a threat to their political and social dominance.

The End of Heretics and the Beginning of Enthusiasts and Cults

"The law knows no heresy," declared the U.S. Supreme Court in 1871. This is the simplest expression of the idea, formed during the Reformation and universalized during the Enlightenment, that everyone is free to believe and practice any religion (or no religion) as they see fit. By the end of the eighteenth century, it was no longer a crime in most Western countries to hold "false beliefs" or to promote those beliefs. But if the concept of heresy was no longer tenable in the public sphere, the rationale behind it was still there: the construction of religious identity, fear of the other, and maintaining boundaries through social control. At the same time, the new sciences of psychology and modern medicine were advancing authoritative explanations for all sorts of human behavior. The new concepts that arose to replace "heresy" depended upon these sciences.

In the seventeenth century, "enthusiasm" became a popular explanation for the existence of dangerous or evil religions. The word "enthusiasm" literally means to be possessed by God, but it came to refer to a religion born from false experience (rather than false belief, as in heresy). To be enthusiastic is therefore to receive religious inspiration from an improper source, one not divine but pathological—in short, to be delusional. The charge of enthusiasm was leveled against many Protestant denominations including Puritans, Anabaptists, Quakers, and later Methodists.

By the nineteenth century, the term enthusiasm had been replaced with one with a more scientific tone: "religious insanity." This was a clinical term for a "disease" caused by exposure to alternative religions, and accounted for the physical behavior—such as barking, shouting, jerking, and dancing—produced by evangelical, often Methodist, revivals of the era. There was a class-based element to the diagnosis of religious insanity. Mental health professionals were generally members of both "mainstream" religions and high socio-economic class. They worried that these revivals were harmful to the lower classes. Like the twentieth-century parents who had their "brain-washed" children kidnapped from cults and deprogrammed, nineteenth-century families used the "religious insanity" rationale to medically incarcerate any of their children who were members of new religions.

Development of the modern cult stereotype in nineteenth-century America

The Puritans' intolerance notwithstanding, the United States has on the whole been particularly welcoming to minority religious groups from all over the world seeking freedom to practice their religion. And of course, many homegrown New Religious Movements have flourished on American soil, and most have lived relatively unscathed. Perhaps inevitably, such a welcoming environment for religious experimentation can lead to a backlash. From the early eighteenth century onwards religious communes as well as revivalist camp meetings were accused of unorthodoxy and sexual license. But it was in the 1830s and 1840s that the "cult" stereotype took something of its present form, including notions of mind control, financial fraud, and violence. The targets of these accusations were not the fringe religions one might think of, but rather organizations that implicitly challenged American political and social values and therefore questioned the social structure.

One of these organizations was the Freemasons. Founded in early eighteenth-century England, Masonic lodges functioned as gentlemen's social clubs (albeit clubs with "secret" initiations, each with enacted myths of journeys, ordeals, and deaths). Lodges spread across Europe and the American colonies in the mid-eighteenth century, and by the 1830s, anti-Masonic literature was painting Masonry as a conspiracy with nefarious origins. The Anti-Mason Party became a powerful political organization for about a decade.

But as historian Philip Jenkins put it, "the largest and most potent anticult movement in American history" was American prejudice against Catholicism.[5] As the Catholic population of North America grew because of immigration from Ireland and later from southern and eastern Europe, Protestants had to confront America's changing religious landscape. Many reacted with fear. Newspaper editorials demonizing Catholics incited riots. Nunneries and abbeys were seen as secretive, depraved, and fundamentally undemocratic. Popular anti-Catholicism was fueled by "atrocity tales" told by supposed former priests or nuns. The most famous of these tales was the best-selling *Awful Disclosures of Maria Monk* (1836), a proven forgery still in print, which describes how priests forced nuns into lewd and depraved acts in a Montreal convent.

In general, anti-Catholicism held that Catholics were obedient only to authoritarian and corrupt bishops and loyal only to the Pope in Rome; Catholicism thus opposed the American value of liberty. Jenkins argues that "all the later anticult images were present here: Catholics exemplified mindless obedience to a deceitful religious leader, and authority was founded upon blood thirsty enforcement."[6]

Next to Catholicism, Mormonism was the most vilified religion of the nineteenth century. The early Mormon community was persecuted as it moved from New York to Ohio to Illinois, and finally to Utah. The LDS Church's growing numbers, financial prosperity, and separatist tendencies made it suspicious in the eyes of its neighbors. Shortly after the founder of the Church, the prophet Joseph Smith, announced his candidacy for president of the United States, he was murdered by a mob. When the LDS Church established the independent State of Deseret in the Utah territory and began publicly to practice the doctrine of polygamy, anti-Mormon sentiment only increased. The U.S. government enacted anti-polygamy laws and enforced them by sending troops to the Utah territory, where they would skirmish with Mormon outposts.

The birth of the tabloid newspaper in the late nineteenth century created a new market for stories about the aberrant behavior of strange, new religions. After Joseph Pulitzer bought the *New York World* in 1883, and William Randolph Hearst bought the *New York Journal* in 1895, sensationalist journalism became a lucrative feature of the American media. Both these newspapers increased their circulation by printing long-running exposés of eccentric religions, which were often just excuses for giving extended treatment to tales of exotic depravity. Other major newspapers soon joined these "pioneers" in providing lurid coverage of financial and sexual misconduct (especially involving underage girls) by leaders of fringe religious groups. For example, in 1894 when Michael Mills, the leader of a new religion based in Detroit called House of David, was charged with statutory rape during a religious ritual, the Detroit and Chicago newspapers had a ready supply of headlines.

The Christian Countercult Movement

The modern "cult" stereotype is clearly indebted to late nineteenth-century mass-media coverage. Another important factor is what sociologists have termed the "Christian countercult movement." In fact, it was this movement that, in the late nineteenth century, first used the word "cult" to mean a religious group that deviates from orthodox Christianity. (The standard meaning of the word "cult" is a system of worship, rites, and ceremonies; it is often used, for example, to describe the religious practices of classical Greece and Rome.)

The countercult movement employed the word "cult" to describe contemporary religious groups it considered "heretical." In the late nineteenth century, Spiritualism, Christian Science, **Jehovah's Witnesses**, and the LDS Church were all deemed heretical by the Christian countercult movement, and were accused (much like ancient or medieval heretics) of taking a piece of true Christianity, perverting it, and preaching false doctrine while proclaiming it the truth. Unlike the mainstream media, the countercult movement is less interested in lurid gossip about "cults" than in a point-by-point refutation of their doctrine. Over the years, the countercult movement has collected a great deal of useful data about "cults," especially the groups named above, which were thought to be "stealing" members from mainstream churches.

The countercult movement has wielded considerable influence on the perception of new religions because its texts are so widely disseminated. Notably, the **Reformed** theologian Jan Van Baalen's *The Chaos of the Cults*, first published in 1938, and the American evangelical Walter Martin's *Kingdom of the Cults*, written in 1965, have both been through many editions and are still in print today. For Martin, any religions that deviated from his definition of biblical Christianity constituted a cult. For many years these books, and a few others like them, were the only sources of information on New Religious Movements available in libraries and bookstores, despite the fact that these works are written from an extremely conservative Protestant perspective. Today, the countercult movement produces a constant stream of books, pamphlets, and audiovisual material, available at all Christian bookstores. Its analysis of NRMs is often informed by its biblical literalism, for example by viewing the New Age movement (as described in the next chapter) as satanically inspired.

CLOSE-UP

The Unification Church

The Unification Church (UC) is the name commonly given to the Holy Spirit Association for the Unification of World Christianity, which is also sometimes known as the Family Federation for World Peace and Unification. The group is best known, however, as "The Moonies," one of the most controversial NRMs to emerge in the latter half of the twentieth century. The Moonies were accused of engaging in many stereotypical "cult" activities, including brainwashing young people (the fact that the UC originates in Korea may be more than a coincidence). The Moonies were also known for recruiting new members through deceptive "front" organizations. In the early 1970s, exposés about the UC began to appear in the mass media, including the magazines *Time* and *Esquire*, and a number of nonfiction books. The 1981 Canadian film *Ticket to Heaven* deals with similar subject matter. These exposés were essentially rescue tales, similar in structure to the anti-Catholic tracts of 150 years earlier. In a prominent 1977 court case in California, parents of adult members of the Unification Church were granted conservatorship (legal guardianship for those deemed mentally unfit) of their children, although the decision was overturned on appeal. These UC members were "deprogrammed" by Steven Hassan, a former Moonie who today remains a prominent anticult activist. Why would an NRM that has never had more than seven or eight thousand members, and has a rather high turnaround rate, attract such negative attention?

One reason is the reputation of the founder, the Reverend Sun Myung Moon. Born in 1920 in what is today North Korea, Moon as a child attended services at the local Presbyterian mission and at sixteen first claimed direct communication with Jesus. He was arrested for preaching in North Korea and was put into a prison camp, from which United Nations forces liberated him. He founded the Unification Church in 1954 in South Korea, where it became officially legal in 1963.

Although the Unification Church gained its first converts in the United States as early as 1959, it was not until the early 1970s that a national Unification movement emerged, with young members living communally and proselytizing intensely. Also during that time Moon became one of the most controversial figures associated with New Religious Movements. His extremely conservative and anti-Communist views led him to support President Nixon during the Watergate affair, to donate large sums to right-wing causes, and to finance the conservative newspaper *The Washington Times*. Moon was head not only of the Unification Church but of several corporations as well. He was convicted of tax evasion in 1982, and later jailed. To some his conviction smacked of religious persecution, and many other religious organizations came to his defense.

The practices and mentality of the Unification Church are quite eclectic, owing something to Korean shamanism and to Confucianism (particularly in its patriarchal values). But Moon sees his organization as an **ecumenical** Christian church, dedicated to overcoming denominational quarrels. Active today in almost 150 countries around the world, the UC has always emphasized internationalism and its most famous ritual celebrates just that: mass wedding ceremonies in which couples of different ethnicities and nationalities are married to each other by Reverend Moon. Scholars have noted that in these "blessing ceremonies," the same couples are married over and over, in an effort publicly to exaggerate the number of active members in the Church.

Some observers analyze the Unification Church as a Korean answer to the Protestant churches that have so aggressively missionized Korea.

The Reverend Sun Myung Moon and his wife Hak Ja Han wear their "Crowns of Peace" to conduct a "blessing ceremony," the mass marriage ritual that is the most important ceremony in the Unification Church.

The UC posits that Korea is the Promised Land and that the savior is Korean. But the UC's theology is more than just a geographic displacement of traditional Christianity. Moon teaches that Satan is alive and holds the world in captivity because of Adam and Eve's false love. Jesus was the second Adam, but he died before he could take a consort, leaving his mission of salvation unfulfilled. Reverend Moon is today's messiah, the third Adam, and along with his wife, he functions as the "True Parents" for all humanity. To be married by Moon is to become part of his holy family.

The Current Anticult Movement

The anticult movement (ACM) is the name given by NRM scholars to the several private organizations dedicated to combating the influence of new religions that they determine are harmful to individuals and societies at large. The ACM in its present form began in the United States and Canada in the 1970s, and today has powerful influence on policy-making towards NRMs around the world. Although the ACM owes much to the Christian countercult movement, it is fundamentally different in that it is secular: its opposition to NRMs is based on the charge not of religious error but of social and psychological danger.

Although one can find cycles of "cult" growth and anticult reactions dating from the nineteenth century, the modern anticult movement grew very specifically out of the social upheaval of the late 1960s. The growing visibility of new religions and the explosion of youth-oriented counter-culture at that time made for a great deal of religious experimentation which in turn led to stories of young people flocking *en masse* to dangerous "cults" such as the **Unification Church** (the Moonies), Scientology, and the Hare Krishnas. Parents concerned that their children were being seduced by exotic new faiths started informal networks, which became the grassroots of the professional anticult movement. The first organized ACM was called Free the Children of God (FREECOG) and was formed in 1972 in opposition to the Children of God, a Christian communal movement, now called the Family. FREECOG later widened its focus to oppose a variety of cults, and changed its name to the Citizens Freedom Foundation, which later became known as the Cult Awareness Network (CAN).

In the 1990s, CAN was sued by a young man who, after joining a **Pentecostal** church, was forcibly deprogrammed by someone his parents had found on the CAN website. Scientologists paid the man's legal fees. The suit was successful: both the deprogrammer and CAN were found guilty of conspiring to violate the man's religious freedom. CAN was forced to pay damages and declared bankruptcy. In an ironic twist, CAN's name, archives, and phone number were taken over by the Church of Scientology. CAN's bankruptcy leaves International Cultic Studies Association (ICSA) as the most significant ACM today. Formerly known as the American Family Foundation, ICSA publishes journals and sponsors conferences that advance their anticult position.

Brainwashing

The brainwashing hypothesis is the most important theoretical contribution made by the anticult movement to the study of New Religious Movements. Brainwashing is best defined as indoctrination through techniques of psychological manipulation, including isolation and repetitive behavior. Brainwashing explains why people might join a religious group they would not otherwise join.

The word "brainwashing" entered the English language in the 1950s as a literal translation of the Chinese word *xi nao*, which refers to a systematic program of thought reform in Communist China used to break "feudal" habits. The Communist "brainwashing" techniques were used to explain the treasonous behavior of a few American soldiers captured by North Koreans during the Korean War. This idea was extended to cults.

But some scholars questioned the ACM's use of the brainwashing hypothesis. Even if it were possible for prisoners of war to be brainwashed through incarceration and torture, NRMs have never been accused of such actions. Certainly, NRMs may exercise considerable influence over their members, but no more so than mainstream religions, or corporations, or educational or military institutions. Studies have found that most people who come into contact with New Religious Movements do not join them, and of those that do, most leave voluntarily after a year or two. In other words, if NRMs do practice "brainwashing," they are not very good at it.

Despite a lack of empirical evidence against brainwashing, the brainwashing concept still has supporters, though they may use different terminology to describe the process. Most scholars remain suspicious of the hypothesis. As sociologist Jeffrey Hadden put it:

> "Brainwashing" is not a viable concept to describe the dynamics of affiliation with new religions. Defenders of "brainwashing" have used other concepts like "mind control" and "thought reform," but they have failed to produce a scholarly literature to support their claims. Thus, whatever euphemisms may be employed, the basic conclusion against the brainwashing thesis is not altered.[7]

Why, then, is the brainwashing theory so persistent, and seemingly so sensible? Brainwashing is so important to the anticult movement because it "medicalizes" what would otherwise be an issue of religious freedom. With brainwashing as an explanation, the ACM can use the judicial and legislative system to combat NRMs, by suing them and by introducing bills to allow parents to have guardianship over their adult children, respectively.

Beyond the professional ACM, brainwashing remains a widespread explanation for the popularity of NRMs—perhaps because the theory so conveniently accounts for why people would believe such outlandish ideas. According to proponents of the brainwashing theory, nobody in their right mind would believe that a Korean businessman is a manifestation of the divine, or that UFOs will soon whisk the chosen few off the planet. One would have to be bamboozled or manipulated to believe in such nonsense. The perceived danger of holding false beliefs stands at the root of the brainwashing hypothesis: the accusation of brainwashing is similar to the age-old charge of heresy. The psychologist Margaret Thaler Singer (1921–2003), the most famous proponent of the brainwashing theory, expressed its main argument thus: "[Cults] prey on the most lonely, vulnerable people they can find, cage you with your own mind through guilt and fear, cut you off from everyone … they don't need armed guards to keep you. Liars, tricksters, it's been the same ever since Eve got the apple, and I doubt it will ever change. They're all basically, really the same, con men."[8]

Almost two thousand years earlier, Bishop Irenaeus, a second-century Christian polemicist, had written in similar terms about heresy: "Error, indeed, is never set forth in its naked deformity, lest, being thus exposed, it should at once be detected. But it is craftily decked out in an attractive dress, so as, by its outward form, to make it appear to the inexperienced (ridiculous as the expression may seem) more true than the truth itself."[9]

In Chapter 1, I argued that New Religious Movements resemble their "parent religion" more than they do other NRMs. But many of the best-known NRMs do not descend from any of the major "world religions." What is the "parent religion" of Theosophy, Scientology, and most New Age groups? These NRMs derive from an alternative

tradition, which runs parallel to the dominant Western ideology. This counter-tradition is neither continuous nor self-conscious and thus has no name; or rather it has several, including metaphysics, Gnosticism, **Hermeticism**, and **Occultism**. No one term is completely accurate, but perhaps the most useful is "Western esotericism."

The esoteric tradition incorporates hundreds of discrete groups, which have existed over thousands of years. What could they have in common? In a sentence, if the dominant Western ideology (including modern science, most Western philosophy, and mainstream Christianity and Judaism) sees humans as limited and separate, the esoteric tradition sees the possibility of humans transcending all limits, and becoming one with the divine. Indeed, in the esoteric worldview, humanity *is* divine, although it has forgotten, lost, or been separated from that divine connection. Most esoteric traditions teach that our link to divinity can be recovered through "special knowledge" (or "gnosis"), taught by trans-human beings. This step-by-step instruction results in personal transformation.

The dominant worldview sees matter and spirit as separate entities. The one or the other may be preferred depending on the particular viewpoint: modern science and materialist philosophy (i.e. Marxism), for example, are concerned with matter and ignore spirit; whereas Christianity tends to glorify spirit, seen as pure, and devalue matter, deemed corrupt. The esoteric worldview, by contrast, sees matter and spirit as a continuum, often expressed as a series of emanations or vibrations. Thus, many esoteric currents include a strong mystical component, emphasizing a direct personal experience of divine encounter. These basic beliefs can be seen in many current NRMs—including Mormonism, Theosophy, most New Age movements, and Scientology. Similarly, the organizational structure of many NRMs derives from esotericism: a series of ascending levels, each one with its own symbolic vocabulary, and reached through a ritual of initiation. This chapter presents a quick historical tour of the Western esoteric tradition, concentrating especially on those aspects with relevance to contemporary NRMs.

The Ancient and Medieval Worlds

Many classical Greek and Roman philosophers had distinctly mystical views. In particular, Platonic idealism, which held that material objects were merely shadows of perfect ideas, was adapted into the philosophical mysticism of Neoplatonism. The preeminent Neoplatonist was Plotinus (204–270 C.E.) who posited the existence of "the One," a single source from which the entire cosmos emanates and with which individual souls should strive to be united.

The first few centuries of the common era (approximately the same time that Neoplatonism was flourishing in the Egyptian city of Alexandria) saw the growth of a number of religious sects that later scholars gave the common name of Gnosticism (a modern term taken from the Greek *gnosis*, "to know"). Gnostic groups might be pagan, Jewish, or Christian in origin, and had many differences in belief and practice, but they all shared the Judeo-Christian theology of fall and redemption. In Gnosticism, however, humans have fallen not because of sin but because of lack of knowledge about our true nature and the evil nature of the world; indeed our original sin is to have forgotten the divine sparks that exist within us. Our salvation lies in recovering this knowledge.

Gnosticism is perhaps the single most important ancient strand contributing to today's esoteric NRMs. For example, Gnostics taught a different tradition about the life, teachings, and nature of Jesus from early mainstream Christianity, which the Gnostics developed both from alternative interpretations of New Testament passages and from the apocryphal gospels (testaments about Jesus which were excluded from the final New Testament). Today, alternative traditions about Jesus are an important element in many NRMs. Another continuity lies in the Gnostic belief that divine light was imprisoned in gross matter, which has parallels in the way light is thought about through-out modern esotericism. Finally, Gnostics, because of their belief that the material world was created by lesser, insane, or evil deities, often had an extremely pessimistic view towards their physical existence, often desiring to remove themselves entirely from time and space. This dualistic tendency was all too evident in the tragic ends of two esoteric NRMs, the Solar Temple and Heaven's Gate, which will be discussed later in this chapter.

The fourth-century establishment of Christianity as the official religion of the Roman empire did not stamp out the esoteric currents of the ancient world. The Cathars and other Christian groups that were condemned as heretical in medieval times, as we saw in the last chapter, can be seen as continuations of Gnostic communities. Medieval chivalric orders such as the Knights Templars have also contributed to the continuation of the esoteric tradition. These orders played important roles during the Crusades but, after amassing considerable fortunes and being accused of political subversion and religious heresy, were persecuted to extinction in the fourteenth century. The story of the Templars and their legendary secrets has been a continuing source of inspiration for European esotericists (as well as conspiracy theorists).

As Christian missionaries spread their religion through Europe during the Middle Ages, another, quite different strand was being woven into the fabric of the Western esoteric tradition: the indigenous religions of the Celtic, Germanic, and Norse people. These traditions, based on seasonal cycles and intimate contact with supernatural beings, survived underground in some form or another even when Christianity had become the official religion across the continent. Some have speculated that the remnants of these traditions survived as medieval and early modern **witchcraft**. It should be noted that what we know of these medieval "esoteric groups"—both heretics and witches—comes from hostile accounts, including unfriendly histories, trial transcripts, and forced confessions. The Middle Ages also saw the zenith of the development of the Cabala, a Jewish system of mysticism, which read numerological and esoteric meanings in the Bible and posited a cosmology based on divine emanations. Cabalistic knowledge was transmitted from a rabbi to a small group of pupils. When, during the Renaissance, certain Christians adapted the Cabala for their own mystical purposes, it would herald a rebirth of the esoteric tradition.

From Renaissance to Enlightenment

The European Renaissance, beginning in the fourteenth century, is best known for the rediscovery of the classical philosophy and values of ancient Greece and Rome. Esotericism also experienced a revival during the Renaissance, resulting in a body of literature that is as profound as it is daunting to study. Alchemists, magicians, and metaphysicians wrote voluminous tomes that are pored over to this day. They transformed Gnostic philosophy, so often pessimistic and dualistic, into the optimistic and expansive doctrine of correspondence. This idea holds that all processes, from chemical transformations to the movements of the stars, and certainly including human affairs, are intimately connected in "a great chain of being." "As above, so below," the saying went—and still goes, for this doctrine underlies many contemporary concerns, such as holistic healing and astrology, as well as, of course, the worldview of many NRMs.

The outstanding figure in Renaissance esotericism was Paracelsus (1493–1541), a true "Renaissance man"—he was a magician, healer, seeker of secret knowledge, and famed exponent of the power of imagination. One hundred years later the Paracelsian tradition was continued by Jacob Boehme (1575–1624), a German shoemaker, who added a deeply personal, mystical spirituality to the Renaissance esoteric world. Paracelsus was probably the inspiration for Christian Rosenkreutz (meaning "Rosy Cross"), the wandering knight of the Fama, a fictional tale that appeared in Germany in 1614. The tale purported to reveal the existence of an ancient esoteric fraternity, the Rosicrucians, whose members supposedly included Egyptian pharaohs, Greek philosophers, King Solomon, and Jesus. **Rosicrucianism** has since been a name chosen by various esoteric groups over the years.

The eighteenth-century Enlightenment, with its emphasis on reason and science, saw the emergence of a new form of esotericism that drew on developments in natural science and technology. Two trained scientists, Swedenborg and Mesmer, exemplified this confluence. Emanuel Swedenborg (1688–1772) is the most important link between the Renaissance and the esoteric NRMs of the nineteenth and twentieth centuries. An engineer, Swedenborg worked for the Royal Swedish Department of Mines while at the same time studying history and theology, including Gnostic texts. At age fifty-five he had a series of mystical visions of various cosmic realms, which he described in minute detail in his popular book, *Heaven and Hell.* As Robert Ellwood and Harry Partin point out, a number of distinct Swedenborgian ideas have today become tenets of esoteric NRMs, including a belief in our spiritual existence before and after earthly life, the possibility of communication with people on "the other side," and the notion (first espoused in the Renaissance) that God's consciousness is continuous with man's.[1]

Franz Anton Mesmer (1734–1815) was an Austrian physician to whom we owe the word "mesmerize." Mesmer's contribution to the esoteric tradition came from his work on the spiritual nature of healing. After experimenting with magnets and hypnotism, he announced the discovery of a universal life force or energy, the imbalance of which in the body causes all illness.

Mesmer and Swedenborg's ideas soon became popular in the United States, which indeed had embraced the European esoteric tradition ever since its early days of colonization. We tend to characterize the Puritans of seventeenth-century New England as rational and hard-working, pious, and dour, and apt to burn witches. In fact, many Puritans practiced magic. Early New England's best-selling books were tales of strange events and almanacs, which were essentially astrological compendia. Indeed, right up until the end of the eighteenth century, astrology was used in medicine, farming, and weather prediction, and alchemy was widely accepted. Puritans were obsessed with signs and portents—strange weather, monstrous births—which reflected a continuation of the basic esoteric cosmology of correspondence. After the American Revolution (1775–1783), while astrology and fortune-telling persisted, European immigrants brought new occult theories, including those of Swedenborg and Mesmer, to America.

NRMs in the Nineteenth Century

Mormonism

The Church of Jesus Christ of the Latter-day Saints, also known as Mormonism, founded in 1830, is arguably the largest esoteric movement in the world. As we saw in Chapter 1, the Church appears to be middle-class and conservative, its political profile more aligned with evangelical Christians than with any New Age or occult group. Yet its history and theology show Mormonism to be part of the alternative tradition. The Mormon esoteric background derives in part from American folk magic. For example, the founder of Mormonism, Joseph Smith (1805–1844), used seer stones to seek buried treasure and later employed those same stones to interpret the mysterious words, found on golden plates, that became the *Book of Mormon*.

Further, the Mormon temple endowment ceremony strongly resembles Masonic initiation rites. Some scholars have argued that the LDS Church merely copied the rituals of Freemasonry. Regardless of its origin, Mormon theology has distinct Gnostic elements: Mormons hold that there are many universes, each with a creator God, and that all humans can become gods. As Mormonism has become part of the American mainstream, the LDS Church has attempted to play down the magical elements of Smith and other early figures, as well as the Gnostic aspects of Mormon theology.

Spiritualism

In 1848 in upstate New York, the Fox sisters, age eight and eleven, began hearing noises that they interpreted as being from the spirit world. News of their ability spread, sparking thousands to experiment with contacting the dead. Most of us are familiar with the séance: a group of people holding hands sitting at a round table. One person, the medium, contacts the spirits of a dead relative of someone at the table. This was the primary practice of Spiritualism, an outlet of the esoteric tradition that was democratic, expansive, and quintessentially American.

Spiritualism had no secret lodges or arcane philosophy but was unashamedly occult, being concerned with the spirits of the dead and the various levels of heaven. These were detailed in the numerous Spiritualist newspapers and lecture series. The most famous lecturer on the Spiritualist circuit was Andrew Jackson Davis (1826–1910), known as the "Seer of Poughkeepsie," who would communicate onstage with the spirits of Benjamin Franklin and Indian chiefs, among others.

Spiritualism saw itself as a scientific religion, in harmony with the latest developments and discoveries such as electricity and ether. Spiritualists rejected the distinction between natural and supernatural, seeing spirits as part of the natural world. Furthermore, they saw the spirit world as a revealed order of concentric spheres, structured hierarchically, almost bureaucratically. In many ways, then, Spiritualism looks back to earlier esoteric movements while anticipating New Age NRMs.

Theosophy

Theosophy was founded by an unlikely pair: Henry S. Olcott (1832–1907), an American lawyer and army colonel, and Helena P. Blavatsky (1831–1891), a mysterious and talkative Russian. In New York City in 1875, they created the Theosophical Society, which would have a profound impact on future esoteric movements. The two met while attending a séance in Vermont, and in many ways Theosophy began as an elite rendition of Spiritualism.

While Spiritualists sought guidance from departed relatives and American worthies, Theosophists received their otherworldly wisdom from the Ascended Masters, a hierarchically organized assemblage of spiritually advanced beings devoted to the betterment of humanity. Significantly, the masters were mostly of Eastern origin and were sometimes seen to congregate in Tibet. Thus the Theosophical Society was seminal in popularizing the idea of Tibet as a repository for spiritual wisdom. While introducing Asian religious ideas into American culture, Theosophists were at the same time giving certain Asians new pride in their own traditions, a subject that will be taken up in the next chapter. Theosophy also popularized many other ideas, such as the lost continent of Atlantis, the mysteries of Egypt, and the spiritual evolution of the earth and humanity.

Blavatsky's 1,300-page masterwork, *The Secret Doctrine*, written in 1888, was inspired by information communicated to Blavatsky by the Ascended Masters in the form of materialized letters. A commentary on an imaginary scripture called "The Stanzas of Dzyan," *The Secret Doctrine* attempts to reconstitute a universally diffused religion. A blend of esoteric Buddhism, Hinduism, Cabala, and quasi-science, *The Secret Doctrine* covers age-old Gnostic themes: it tells that humans were once spiritual beings, and can be again. According to Theosophists, the book itself represents the restoration of a divine truth once fragmented.

Mind Cure movements

The Maine clockmaker Phineas Quimby (1802–1866), as the first European American healer who believed that all physical diseases or ailments could be cured by harnessing one's mental and spiritual powers, can be considered the father of the Mind Cure movement, which includes both New Thought and Christian Science. Indeed, Quimby has been called the founder "of the whole so-called Metaphysical Movement in America."[2] In 1862 he treated Mary Baker Eddy

(1821–1910), who went on to write *Science and Health with Key to the Scripture*, seen by Christian Scientists as a companion volume to the Bible. In 1879 she founded the First Church of Christ, Scientist.

Like Theosophy, Christian Science owes much to Spiritualism, mesmerism and Swedenborg, yet it took these currents in a very different direction—one focused not on esoteric cosmology but on healing, and using mind as the controlling factor of reality. As we saw in the last chapter, the early anticult movement attacked Christian Science. Today, however, the Church's image is about as far away from a "dangerous cult" as can be—its membership is mostly wealthy and aging, and is on the decline; while its daily newspaper, the *Christian Science Monitor*, is respected for its unbiased coverage of international affairs. But Christian Science still arouses controversy for its exclusive reliance on silent prayer to cure illness. Parents who have refused to administer conventional medicine to their dying children have been legally prosecuted.

Emma Curtis Hopkins (1849–1925) had studied Christian Science with Eddy in Boston and was the first editor of the monthly magazine the *Christian Science Journal*, but she was excommunicated from the Church by the famously authoritarian Eddy in 1885. In Chicago, Hopkins founded a theological seminary and newsletter that became the seeds of the New Thought movement. Her students went on to found most of the denominations (such as Unity, Religious Science, and Divine Science) that are still operative today and make up the International New Thought Alliance. Like Christian Science, New Thought emphasizes the spiritual healing of biological disease. But New Thought also focused on curing the disease of poverty— thus teaching how to achieve wealth through esoteric means. New Thought also differs from Christian Science in that it is less specifically Christian and more open to other religious traditions.

New Thought decisively wed the esoteric doctrine of the continuity of matter and spirit to American optimism and Victorian sentimentality. As an example, here is Ella Wheeler Wilcox (1855–1919), one of the nineteenth century's most popular poets and a New Thought advocate:

> Words are great forces in the realm of life.
> Be careful of their use. Who talks of hate,
> Poverty, of sickness, but sets rife
> These very elements to mar his fate.[3]

Although public lectures at New Thought churches are still announced in the religion listings of daily newspapers, the New Thought world-view, around the turn of the twentieth century, largely became diffused into everyday culture, losing its specific terminology ("All-Supply," "the Uncreated") on its way to becoming the "power of positive thinking" self-help movement.

Where are the nineteenth-century new religions now?

All of these nineteenth-century "esoteric" NRMs spread internationally, and continue to exist today. The Mormon Church is by far the largest of these, with a current membership of over ten million; it is actively propagated worldwide, in the face of continued attacks by the evangelical countercult movement, which sees it as occult and non-Christian. Spiritualism enjoyed success in the U.K. and France, and now has significant influence among the new religions of Brazil. From its headquarters in India, Theosophy established centers in all the major European cities. New Thought spread throughout Europe (it was persecuted in Germany by the Nazis in the 1930s and 1940s), South Africa, Australia, and Japan, where it developed into the independent sect Seicho-No-Ie (which currently has over a million members).

Spiritualism, Theosophy, and New Thought exist today in the West as a series of small, fairly complacent organizations. Their importance lies not in their continued institutional presence but in how they transmitted the esoteric tradition into the twentieth century. Many of their ideas and practices have become a familiar part of our culture—from a belief in the beneficial presence of spirits of dead relatives, through the power of positive thinking, to the use of Hindu vocabulary. And of course they all influenced specific NRMs of the twentieth century.

Esotericism in Twentieth-Century NRMs

European currents

In early twentieth-century Britain, interest in the esoteric manifested itself through a proliferation of Theosophical lodges as well as groups devoted to "ceremonial magick" (often pronounced MAGE-ick; the "k" is to distinguish it from conjuring tricks). Magick, in common with esotericism in general, purports that unseen powers or energies affect our physical world. Unlike most esoteric movements, however, magick groups endeavor to harness those powers by the force of will. The best-known magick group was the Hermetic Order of the Golden Dawn, which counted the Irish poet W.B. Yeats (1865–1939) as a member. Most of these orders were quite small, yet they constantly split from each other. Despite their occult (secret) nature, many lodges became quite well known, in large part due to Aleister Crowley (1875–1947), the foremost theoretician of magick and a colorful publicity seeker. As head of the British branch of the Ordo Templo Orientis, he founded new magick temples in North America.

In continental Europe a different flavor of esotericism prevailed. Neo-Templar orders were based on legends of the Knights Templars and the presumed secret they kept about the Holy Grail. By the early 1980s there may have been over one hundred rival orders in Europe, whose interests ranged from apocalypticism to espionage, from sex magic to gastronomy. None was particularly well known until the Order of the Solar Temple (OST) grabbed headlines in 1994 with the murder-suicide of its core membership.

The OST, like other Templar orders, and esoteric NRMs in general, was composed of upper-middle-class, well-educated adults. Mayors, bankers, and corporate managers were among the OST members who perished. Five charred bodies were found in Quebec on October 4, 1994. The following day twenty-three bodies were discovered in Switzerland and later another twenty-five were found. It emerged that "advanced" OST members believed that to progress to their new solar bodies they must "depose" their mortal ones. Less advanced members had to be "helped" out of their mortal bodies. A third class of members, perceived by the OST leadership as traitors, was simply executed.

UFO movements

Another late twentieth-century case of NRM mass suicide is that of Heaven's Gate. In March 1997, all thirty-nine members of the sect committed suicide at their compound near San Diego, California. Like the OST they too took a Gnostic belief to a violent extreme, and killed themselves to rid themselves of their earthly shells. But Heaven's Gate's esoteric expression was of the UFO (unidentified flying object), not the neo-Templar, variety. The passing through the skies of the Hale-Bopp comet, which the group believed concealed an alien spaceship ready to transport them to another planet, precipitated their suicide.

Heaven's Gate was just one of several dozen UFO-inspired NRMs, although the only one to engage in such suicidal behavior. Among the best known are the Raelians, based in Montreal, Canada, and the Aetherius Society, based in London, England. The modern UFO movement began in 1947, the year a man in Washington State reported seeing nine "flying saucers" in the sky, but its roots in esotericism go back further. Emanuel Swedenborg, among his many other fanciful journeys, describes his visits to other planets.

Some UFO groups see aliens from outer space as higher spiritual beings, put on earth to help humanity take the next step forward. This belief is directly influenced by Theosophy's concept of Ascended Masters. Spiritualism has also been an influence on the various UFO groups that receive messages from aliens via telepathic communication. Finally, it should be noted that Christian-influenced UFO groups reconcile interpretation of biblical prophecy with flying saucer activity. In general, UFO-based NRMs look to unite the realms of religion and science, and to make humanity's role in the cosmos central to both realms.

Esotericism meets science

Since the days of Swedenborg and Mesmer, esoteric new religions have often allied themselves with science and technology, feeling that it validates their beliefs while discrediting traditional Christianity. Spiritualism, Mind Cure, and UFO movements have all used scientific language. As psychology emerged as a scientific discipline, it was not only used by opponents of new religions, as seen in the last chapter, but also by the new religions themselves. They found in psychology a new language to express the old idea that humans possessed infinite potential and that our limitations were largely self-imposed. The line between esoteric religion and psychology was blurred even further by the **"human potential" movement**, which emerged during the mid-twentieth century.

Perhaps the best example of an NRM that uses scientific language and "human potential" psychology in the service of an esoteric doctrine is Scientology. In 1950, author L. Ron Hubbard (1911–1986) published an article in a science-fiction magazine that explained a new "science" of Dianetics, which aims to unleash full human potential. Soon after, Hubbard put Dianetics at the center of a more spiritual and esoteric movement which he called Scientology. The first Church of Scientology opened in 1954. Like many esoteric movements,

CLOSE-UP

Channeling Movements

Imagine listening intently to someone speaking on spiritual matters with a voice that is not their own. Or imagine inviting a strange voice to speak through you, using techniques learned from exposure to an esoteric NRM. This widespread phenomenon is known as **channeling**, which might broadly be defined as an individual receiving or transmitting information through an exterior consciousness. By this definition, the oracles and shamans of traditional religions would count as channelers, as would the prophets of revealed religions. The term itself dates to the UFO movement of the 1940s and 1950s, when contactees would claim to have received messages "channeled" from flying saucers. Modern channeling also owes much to Spiritualism and Theosophy.

The era of modern channeling might be said to have begun in 1963, when Jane Roberts (1929–1984), a housewife from New York State, began channeling "Seth." Books by Roberts (writing as Seth), such as *The Nature of Personal Reality* and *Seth Speaks*, have sold in the millions. The most successful channels currently active are J.Z. Knight and Jach Pursel, who channel Ramtha and Lazaris respectively. Both are known as "full trance, objective" channels. "Objective" means that the source (Ramtha or Lazaris) is not a part of the channel's (Knight or Pursel's) consciousness; "full trance" means that the channel is not conscious when the source speaks through him or her. A channel is different from a medium in that the channel is not the intermediary between the consciousness coming through them and the audience. The channel does not remain in a transfixed, altered state while channeling; rather they leave their body completely and allow the consciousness coming through to have full faculty over all their bodily movements and functions.

Ramtha's School of Enlightenment, located in Yelm, Washington, was founded by J.Z. Knight (1946–), a woman who, while a young executive for a cable company, had psychic experiences and saw UFOs. In 1977, while sitting in her kitchen, she saw the giant figure of a man in a beam of purple light. He described himself as Ramtha, a 35,000-year-old Lemurian warrior enslaved by people from Atlantis. Soon after, Ramtha began speaking through J.Z. Knight in what has been described as a medieval, husky voice. Ramtha's theology has much in common with the other esoteric movements described in this chapter. He tells us that humans are gods who have forgotten their divinity and will remember it as they ascend through seven levels of being. Matter, he contends, is concentrated spirit.

In 1974 Jach Pursel (1947–), a Michigan insurance executive, fell asleep during his nightly meditation practice with his wife Penny and began talking in another voice. The speaker identified himself as Lazaris, a "spark of consciousness" beyond our physical and causal planes, who communicates through Jach to help people on this planet reach the next evolutionary step. Pursel set up a non-profit foundation to promote Lazaris's teachings, but in the late 1970s changed this to a for-profit corporation and in 1980 relocated to Marin County, California, a center of New Age activity. In 1986 the organization began to mass-market Lazaris tapes and books through mail order and New Age bookstores. Today,

J.Z. Knight, channel of the 35,000-year-old Lemurian warrior named Ramtha.

people interact with Lazaris via a regular schedule of seminars conducted in hotel meeting rooms in Orlando, a website, and occasional one-on-one phone consultations. At the seminar Lazaris speaks on a predetermined subject, leading a guided meditation and sometimes taking questions from the audience. Topics range from how to release negative ego to how the star Sirius affects our lives.

Both these channeling groups inculcate an esoteric worldview by teaching an eclectic blend of Hindu terminology, speculative history, and popular science. Both operate as corporations that offer "intensive" sessions to hundreds at a time while grossing millions of dollars annually. Still, there are major differences between these two most popular channels. Lazaris speaks on a shifting variety of esoteric topics, whereas Ramtha has a standardized curriculum, beginning with a free introductory video lecture and then a one-week beginners' retreat. Since 1988, in fact, Knight has led a "school" complete with theoretical knowledge and tests in which to apply the knowledge to gain experience and understanding. Ramtha's "great work" involves training the mind by walking though outdoor mazes, looking for a small object on a field while blindfolded, and other physical tests. The Ramtha headquarters in Yelm, Washington has become a permanent training center, and has developed its own set of rituals and spiritual practices. By contrast, Lazaris seminars are neither body-centered nor interactive, and Pursel specifically discourages an independent community.

For every high-end channel there are thousands of small-scale ones, who might channel for a few people at a time and work for free or by donation.

Scientology provides the adherent with a series of attainment levels reached by undergoing secret rites of initiation. Scientologists climb these levels by undoing psychic trauma from previous lives, using a machine known as an E-Meter. While Scientology keeps secret the upper levels of Dianetics, many of the relevant documents have been made available through their being introduced into court transcripts or on the Internet. Thus we know that Scientology's closely guarded creation story resembles that of UFO groups: the alien ruler Xenu killed billions of his alien subjects, whose tormented souls now occupy the bodies of human beings.

Neopaganism

The term "pagan" is derived from the Latin *paganus*, which means "country-dweller." It was the term given by the (mainly) urban early Christians to the (mainly rural) non-Christian communities. Today the term Neopagan is applied to any NRM that gains inspiration from pre-Christian Europe. There exists a wide variety of Neopagan movements, including **Wicca** and other orders of witchcraft, Druidism (a Celtic-inflected Neopaganism), and Norse Neopagans (who often call themselves Heathens). Their shared beliefs and practices include the holding of ceremonies outdoors, a reverence for the Goddess or a god/goddess pair, the practice of magic for beneficial purposes, and a belief in the sacred quality of nature. Many Neopagans share a ritual calendar revolving around eight holidays, determined by the phases of the moon.

Though Neopagans might not see themselves as an "NRM" or as part of the history of esotericism, it is quite clear they came out of the same nineteenth-century esoteric revival that produced the neo-Templars, Rosicrucianism, and ceremonial magick. Neopagans overlap with ceremonial "magicians" in their interest in magic and ritual, and their practice of ritual initiation within esoteric fellowships. One of the largest traditions in Neopaganism, Wicca, was created in the 1950s by an Englishman named Gerald Gardner (1884–1964), who claimed to have been initiated by a traditional English witch. In fact, Gardner adapted Wicca from Crowleyan magick, Freemasonry, and Asian religions. Wicca spread to the United States in the 1970s, and is practiced in all parts of the country today.

Neopagans are sometimes misrepresented (especially by conservative Christian groups) as satanic, in part because they often worship a pre-Christian "horned God" representing fertility, whose iconography became associated with the Devil in medieval Christianity. But Neopagans have nothing to do with Satanism. There are a few modern satanic NRMs in existence, however, although their conception of Satan has less to do with evil than with radical individualism.

The New Age

"New Age" is a nebulous term for a non-denominational esoteric spirituality that was born in the mid-1970s, swept over the Western world through the 1980s, and peaked around the end of that decade. Many scholars contend that the New Age is rooted in the Theosophical tradition, as many New Age NRMs make (often unacknowledged) use of concepts like the "Ascended Masters" and the lost continents of Lemuria and Atlantis.[4] The defining quality of the New Age movement, however, is its eclecticism. Any one New Age group might combine, for instance, Neopaganism, UFO activity, ritual magick, popular psychology, and technological devices. Unique hallmarks of the New Age include a focus on the healing power of pyramids and crystals, which are believed to focus energy and transmit it into one's body, and the practice of channeling (see Close-up, p. 48). The New Age's extreme eclecticism is held together by a belief that the esoteric quest for the perfection of the "higher self" has the power to precipitate social and planetary change.

Another important element of the New Age is its incorporation of Asian religions. Like Theosophy before it, the New Age borrows selective terminology, worldviews, and spiritual techniques from Buddhism, Hinduism, and other Eastern traditions. But the presence of Asian religions in the West is too important to the study of NRMs to be considered as a subset of esotericism. The next chapter looks at this presence.

Many NRMs in the West derive from one or more Asian religious traditions. Hinduism, Buddhism, and **Sikhism** have had the most influence, but **Shinto** and Daoism have had some as well. Notable examples of NRMs in the West that come from Asia include Hare Krishna, Soka Gakkai, and Sikh Dharma.

As we have seen, NRMs are defined by their "otherness," their outsider status. In the last chapter, Western esotericism, shown to be a source of many NRMs, was labeled (or labeled itself) a "counter-tradition" or "alternative worldview" arising from within the heart of the Western tradition. This chapter looks at NRMs that are labeled as unacceptably different because of their origin. They lie outside not only social and religious boundaries but geographical boundaries as well. These NRMs attract public attention in the West because of their "Oriental" external trappings: often the leaders are Asian immigrants; adherents may dress in Asian robes, chant in an Asian language, and worship in temples with Asian architecture and decor. Core beliefs derived from Asian religions, such as reincarnation, karma (the effect that past actions have on one's present and future lives), or the impermanence the self, further mark these NRMs as foreign.

Of course, many of these Asian New Religious Movements are "new" only to the West. Their parent religions have roots that extend back thousands of years. But some Asian NRMs are new in their country of origin, and exist in a state of high tension with the religious and social establishment there.

What accounts for the large number of Asian NRMs active in the West? Certainly, the West has long been fascinated with the East. One does not have to be a scholar of new religions to notice that Asian fashion, food, culture, and philosophy have all impacted the West. The "exotic East" provides an inexhaustible number of fads for Westerners, from eating raw fish to wearing colorful saris. This fascination with the East proceeds on a venerable cycle that is often forgotten, so that each Asian fad seems like an original discovery. So it is with religious and spiritual ideas from the East. Tibetan Buddhism or yoga may seem to have caught the West's attention only in the last ten or twenty years, but historians have shown they held interest for small groups of Westerners over one hundred years ago. What is the source of the continuing appeal?

The psychoanalyst Sigmund Freud (1856–1939) famously theorized religion as a form of wish fulfillment, the purpose of which is to meet humankind's psychological needs. Whatever the merits of that argument, it certainly seems to account in part for the continued appeal of Asian religions in the West. Asian religions' paths to self-knowledge and self-realization act as a corrective to Western scientific materialism on the one hand, and Western religious dogma on the other. For the last few centuries, a steady coterie of Western seekers (of truth, of enlightenment, of escape—or of all of these) has found *something* in the wisdom of the East.

The Missionary Impulse

As well as the deep-seated fascination noted above, another important factor in accounting for the presence of Asian religions in the West is the active role played by Asian religious propagators. Asian religions travel west for the same reason that Christianity goes east: a sense of mission. A "New Religious Movement" from our perspective might look like a foreign mission from another. Any faith that sees itself as embodying a universal truth will tend to propagate itself. This faith will become portable: its sense of the sacred will be found not on a mountain or in a river but in a scripture or a practice that can be transported and translated. The faith will, in short, become a missionary religion. The last half millennium has seen the Christianization of the indigenous population of the Americas. For the last two hundred years Protestant and Catholic missionaries from Europe and North America have been active in almost every nation in Africa, Asia, and the Pacific Islands, often working hand in hand with colonial or commercial interests. But Christianity is not the only missionary religion. Islam became the dominant religion in large parts of Africa and Asia through intense missionary activity. The earliest great missionary religion, however, was Buddhism.

Global Buddhism

From its beginnings in India some 2,500 years ago, Buddhism has proved itself to be easily adaptable yet with an unchanging basic message, promising salvation through enlightenment. Buddhism was the first truly global faith. It spread along the ancient trade routes known as the Silk Road, from India to Central Asia to China, whence Chinese missionaries took it to Korea and Japan, where it is still practiced. As well, Buddhism remains the majority religion in Sri Lanka and Southeast Asia.

As Buddhism spread throughout Asia it initially met with some of the same hostility as that encountered by Asian NRMs today. When Buddhism entered China, in the second and third centuries of the common era, Confucian officials attacked Buddhist monasticism for promoting such deeply un-Chinese practices as cutting off one's hair, leaving one's parents, and renouncing marriage. As Buddhism took hold in Chinese society, Confucians and Daoists continued to attack it, viewing it as a threat to their own religious preeminence. Buddhism has been labeled a "dangerous" and "foreign" religion several times in Chinese and Japanese history, most recently in Japan during the Meiji Restoration (1868–1912). In part because it has never threatened to become a majority religion, Buddhism in North America and Europe has so far received a comparatively warmer reception.

Modern Hinduism

Hinduism is not normally seen as a missionary religion. Indeed there is some argument about whether it is a religion at all. The British coined the word "Hinduism" in the 1820s to designate the range of religious activity of the people of India. Around the same time, in response to Christian missionaries and the spread of Enlightenment ideas, Indian intellectuals consciously set out to define their tradition both as a world religion and as a fundamental of Indian identity. This process resulted in the standardized form of Hinduism prevalent today among the Indian urban middle class. This redefinition of Hinduism resulted in a spate of Hindu reform movements, often modeled on Western denominations. The earliest of these were the Brahmo Samaj ("Divine Society"), founded in 1828, and the Arya Samaj ("Noble Society"), founded in 1875. Both rejected typical Hindu activities because they included the worship of multiple gods. Instead these groups advocated a "return" to the **monism** (the belief that all reality comes from the same source) that they saw in the earliest

Hindu scriptures. The popular holy man Ramakrishna (1836–1886) founded a more devotional modern movement. A priest in a temple to Kali, Ramakrishna claimed numerous personal encounters with this goddess as well as experiences that confirmed for him the validity of all religious traditions. The Ramakrishna movement produced several important missionaries and was a major factor in the spread of Hindu-based NRMs in the West.

The role of the **guru** provides another clue as to how the non-missionary religion of Hinduism could produce so many Western NRMs. In Hinduism "guru" can refer to any religious teacher and many Indians have gurus to help them along their spiritual path. In fact the guru's role is as cultural as it is religious; South Asian Christian leaders may well call themselves gurus and open ashrams (retreat centers). In some forms of Hinduism it is the guru's role to awaken the spiritual energy (called *kundalini, prana*, or *shakti*) in his or her disciples and give them the *shaktipat* (spiritual awakening) experience. This can often be accomplished by a casual touch and can induce mystic vision or transformation in the recipient. The promise of these life-transforming experiences has made for a steady demand of gurus in the West, where increasing numbers of non-Asians have taken on the role of guru within both the Buddhist and the Hindu traditions.

Sikh influences

Another religion in which the "guru" figures prominently is Sikhism. Founded by Guru Nanak (1469–1539) in the Punjab region of India, Sikhism shows the influence of both Islam (in its absolute monotheism) and Hinduism (in its belief in karma and reincarnation). With the exception of Sikh Dharma, to be discussed below, Sikhism functions in the West more as an ethnic religion than as an NRM. However, a lineage of gurus, founded around the same time and place as Sikhism, has had an important, but largely overlooked, influence on NRMs in the West. This lineage, known as the **Sant Mat** tradition, is not an exclusive faith—among its founders were Hindus and Muslims, although most of the gurus in the tradition have been Sikh. Sant Mat gurus are required to spend several hours per day in meditation contemplating the divine sound (known as *Shabd*), the Word that created the universe. Sant Mat devotees refer to both the sacred teachings and the meetings where those teachings are given as *satsangs*. As we will see, several NRMs, such Eckankar and the Divine Light Mission, derive from Sant Mat theology.

East Asian traditions

Daoism and Shinto, the indigenous religions of China and Japan respectively, have had a more subtle impact on NRMs in the West. The word Shinto can be applied to a number of religious activities, including local worship of *kami* (spirits who reside in natural settings) as well as imperial ritual. In the late nineteenth century, State Shinto was invented by the Japanese government to promote nationalistic sentiment. These activities do not translate well outside of Japan, but Shinto has formed the basis for several Japanese NRMs, some of which have a Western presence. These will be discussed in Chapter 5.

There are several teachers of Daoism in the West, from both Chinese and European backgrounds. Some teachers claim to have been initiated into specific Daoist lineages, while others claim to follow the Dao, a more universalist understanding. These teachers have founded practice groups that sometimes have a religious component, but most groups are too diffuse to be considered NRMs. However, Daoism's influence on alternative spirituality in the West, including martial arts, healing, and divination, has been considerable.

Asian "NRMs" in the West Before 1965

Exactly how far back does contact between "East" and "West" go? We know that following Alexander the Great's encounter with Buddhism in North India in the fourth century B.C.E., the Indian King Ashoka sent Buddhist missionaries to Greece. Some speculate that these missionaries may have influenced Western esoteric philosophy. If Neoplatonism and Gnosticism owe something to Buddhism, then would all the esoteric traditions described in the last chapter be Asian at root? This possibility remains conjecture. We do know that Asia has fascinated Europe since at least the time of Marco Polo, the famed twelfth-century traveler. In the eighteenth century important Enlightenment thinkers such as Gottfried Leibniz, Denis Diderot, and Voltaire became intellectually stirred by Chinese philosophy, which they saw as being moral and rational without resorting to superstitious theism (belief in a god or gods). In 1784 British Orientalists formed the Asiatick Society, which produced the first English translation of a Hindu scripture, the Bhagavad-Gita. By the nineteenth century, many European thinkers looked to India as the mystical, organic source of Indo-European culture. Early Buddhist and classical Hindu texts, translated from Sanskrit and Pali, were touted as the source of human religiousness.

These translations made their way to the United States, where they had a profound influence on the emerging Transcendentalist philosophy. Developed by the essayist Henry David Thoreau (1817–1862), the poet Ralph Waldo Emerson (1803–1882), and others, Transcendentalism proposed a spiritual reality that could be known through intuition. Some of its adherents helped found the American Orientalist Society in 1842, and the Transcendentalist periodical *The Dial* went on to print the Lotus Sutra and other Buddhist and Hindu texts. And in 1878, the Transcendentalist Bronson Alcott (1799–1888) published an American edition of *The Light of Asia*, a best-selling biography of the Buddha. It should be noted that neither Emerson nor Thoreau nor Alcott ever met a practicing Buddhist or Hindu from Asia. For them, Asian religions were purely textual phenomena and a long way from anything that could be called an NRM.

Meanwhile, Asians emigrated to the West—beginning in the 1840s with Chinese communities established on the west coast of Canada and the United States—and practiced their religions. The first Chinese temple in the U.S. opened in 1853, the first Japanese Buddhist temple in 1898, the first Shinto temple in 1904, and the first Sikh gurdwara in 1912. These functioned mostly as "ethnic religions," and non-Asian converts were rare. In Europe, immigration restrictions meant that no communities of Buddhist or Hindu immigrants existed before the 1960s.

The World's Parliament of Religions and its Aftermath

In 1880, H.S. Olcott, whom we met in the previous chapter as the co-founder of the Theosophical Society, became the first U.S. citizen formally to convert to Buddhism. He was "taking refuge" in Sri Lanka (known then as Ceylon) at the time, however, and the first Buddhist conversion on U.S. soil did not take place until 1893, following the World's Parliament of Religions in Chicago. Held in conjunction with the Columbian Exposition, the Parliament brought Asian religious leaders to the West to present their religious beliefs on a platform shared with liberal Protestants, Catholics, and Jews. A leading Theosophist, William Q. Judge, was a vice-president.

Swami Vivekananda, the first Hindu missionary to America and a celebrated speaker at the 1893 World's Parliament of Religions. He later founded the Vedanta Society.

The most popular Asian delegate was a young Hindu swami (religious teacher) named Vivekananda (1863–1902), a member of Arya Samaj as well as devotee of Ramakrishna. He presented Hinduism as a religion that was both progressively ecumenical and intensely heartfelt. After the Parliament, Vivekananda, who spoke English with fluency and eloquence, went on a lecture tour of the United States and founded the Vedanta Society, which could be considered the oldest Asian NRM in the West. Today the Vedanta Society has twelve centers and a few thousand members in the United States.

Notable Asian Buddhist leaders were also invited to the Parliament, including Anagarika Dharmapala (1864–1933), a Sri Lankan monk and protégé of Olcott, and Soyen Shaku (1859–1919), a Japanese abbot from the Zen tradition. Zen, a branch of Japanese Buddhism that emphasizes meditation as the way to access directly the experience of enlightenment, would come to have the greatest influence of any form of Buddhism on American culture. Indeed, several of Shaku's disciples emigrated to the United States and established their own schools there. In the wake of the Parliament, Buddhism came to be seen by a small number of open-minded Euro-Americans as a viable life path, not just an exotic philosophy. By the turn of the century, the U.S. was home to perhaps two to three thousand Buddhist converts and tens of thousands more Buddhist sympathizers.

Many Asian religious leaders felt the brunt of the anti-Asian sentiment that was running high at the turn of the twentieth century, which drew little distinction between East and South Asia. The racist term "Yellow Peril" was coined in an American editorial cartoon of 1895, which depicted a monstrous Buddha menacing the West. It referred to the supposed dangers of Japanese and Chinese immigrants, who were seen as unable to assimilate into American culture.

Vivekananda and his successors evoked powerful antipathy from Christian missionaries, who were worried about the spreading of "Hindu heathenism." Popular prejudice held that the swamis mostly attracted rich and gullible women. Nonetheless, other Indian masters followed the path blazed by Vivekananda. Paramhansa Yogananda (1893–1952) came to the U.S. in 1920, founded the Self-Realization Fellowship (SRF), and published a best-selling spiritual memoir, *Autobiography of a Yogi* (1946). By 1937, 150,000 people had taken the Self-Realization Fellowship's initial correspondence course.

Meanwhile, students of Soyen Shaku went on to found Zen Centers in New York, San Francisco, and Los Angeles in the 1920s and 1930s. A new generation of non-Asian Zen leaders studied in Japan in the 1950s. Tibetan Buddhist teachers first came to the West via India, where they fled following the Chinese Communist crackdown on a Tibetan uprising in 1959. The first Western teacher in the Tibetan tradition, Geshe Wangyal (1902–1983), was actually a Mongolian. Settling in New Jersey in 1955, he taught the first generation of Euro-American monks in the Tibetan Buddhist tradition, who went on to found Tibetan Studies programs at U.S. universities.

Asian NRMs in the West: The Post-1965 Boom

In the late 1960s and 1970s the number of Asian-inspired NRMs in the West increased dramatically. This rise is often attributed to the "spiritual hunger" of the hippie/boomer generation. Both mainstream religion and consumer capitalism were seen as empty promises. Disenchanted with Western values, a noticeable minority of Westerners sought an immediate experience of ecstasy or transcendence. Gurus or masters from the East could provide these experiences through techniques of **yoga**, meditation, and chanting, or through direct transmission.

Another explanation for the boom might be cultural preparation. In the 1950s, writers identified with the Beat movement, such as Allen Ginsberg, Gary Snyder, and Jack Kerouac, incorporated Buddhist themes into their poetry and novels. By the late 1960s, Westerners on the whole were sufficiently familiar with Asian ideas to create a natural market for Asian-based NRMs. This familiarity was largely due to the availability of mass-market paperback editions of Asian "spiritual classics," including the Bhagavad-Gita and the Daodejing alongside popularized explanations by authors such as D.T. Suzuki and Alan Watts and an increase in college-level courses.

But perhaps the decisive factor in the increase of Asian NRMs was the change in immigration law in the West, notably the United States' Immigration Act of 1965, which put an end to the national origins quota system that had severely restricted Asian immigration since 1924. Similar reforms took place around the same time in Western Europe and Canada. These changes removed race-based restrictions on immigration and allowed a substantial number of Asians, including spiritual leaders, into the West for the first time.

This shift in immigration policy prompted sociologists Roger Finke and Rodney Stark to argue that a "supply-side" (as opposed to a "demand-side") rationale lay behind the growth of interest in Asian traditions since 1965. According to Finke and Stark, "it was not so much that Eastern faiths suddenly struck a responsive chord in the American counter-culture as that their growth had been artificially thwarted until then."[1] For many reasons, then, the number and variety of Asian "missionaries" sharply increased from the mid-1960s onwards, and show no sign of abating.

Buddhism

Zen Buddhism continued to put down deep roots in Western soil. One of its flagship institutions was the San Francisco Zen Center (SFZC), founded by Shunryu Suzuki (1905–1971). The Zen priest Suzuki came to the U.S. in the late 1950s to head a Japanese-American Zen temple. In 1962 he opened the Zen Center in order to appeal to non-Asian Americans, and SFZC became one of the city's premier spiritual and cultural institutions. Zen meditation groups now practice all over North America and Europe. Another Buddhist meditation technique that gained a foothold in the West is *vipassana*, or insight meditation. The Friends of the Western Buddhist Order, founded in 1967 by an Englishman ordained as a monk, emphasizes *vipassana*. This represents one of Britain's largest Buddhist movements.

Lamas (Tibetan Buddhist monks) representing all the denominations of Tibetan Buddhism were teaching in the West by the late

1960s. Of these, Chogyam Trungpa (1939–1987) was the best known. His fame came in part from the institutions he built: not only Dharmadhatu (the international headquarters of which are in Halifax, Canada), a religious organization which follows his own lineage, but also Shambhala International, a non-sectarian training program, and the Naropa Institute in Boulder, Colorado, the first Buddhist university in the West. The other source of Chogyam Trungpa's fame was his outsize personality, which included occasional drunkenness and sexual promiscuity. Whether these habits demonstrated his own spiritual enlightenment, which gave him license to transcend conventional morality, or whether they were simply bad character traits, is a matter still being discussed in the American Buddhist community. But there is no doubt that, from his arrival in the U.S. in 1970 until his death, Trungpa was one of the most fascinating of the "guru" figures in the history of Asian NRMs in the West.

Hinduism

One of the best-known post-1965 Hindu gurus is Maharishi Mahesh Yogi (1917?–), the man responsible for bringing Transcendental Meditation (TM) to the West. After founding his organization in 1957, he opened branches in the U.S. in 1959 and in Britain a year later, gaining the notice of the world-famous pop group, the Beatles, and other media celebrities. TM involves meditating twice a day for twenty minutes, on a mantra (word with sacred power) given by the instructor. One of the keys to TM's success was that it did not require joining a new religion or leaving one's own faith. By the late 1960s, the basic TM course was said to have been taken by a million people. Taught in public schools and corporate boardrooms, TM was, for a time, the most widely marketed system of meditation. The Maharishi's organization now encompasses Maharishi International University in Iowa and the Natural Law political party. Recently, the TM organization has become interested in traditional Indian medicine, known as ayurveda. The famous "New Age" healer Deepak Chopra (1947–) was trained in Western medicine but became interested in meditation and ayurveda after meeting the Maharishi in 1985. Although Chopra still refers to the Maharishi as his mentor, he is no longer affiliated with his organization.

Contrasting with the impersonal transmission of TM, several Hindu-based NRMs emphasized that spiritual enlightenment could only be attained through a face-to-face encounter with the guru. Those

CLOSE-UP

Soka Gakkai

Every day, thousands of people in the Western world chant the *daimoku*, a phrase that sounds like "nam-myo-ho-renge-kyo" and literally means "Praise to the wonderful Lotus Sutra." Many do so in front of a *gohonzon*, a scroll with those same words written in Japanese calligraphy. This chanting remains the primary religious activity of Soka Gakkai, a worldwide Buddhist lay movement based in Japan. Soka Gakkai is thus very different from most other Buddhist NRMs in the West, which typically emphasize silent meditation. Soka Gakkai, which means Value Creation Society, was founded in 1937 as an educational reform movement (inspired by American sociology and pragmatic philosophy). Later, it affiliated with Nichiren Shoshu, a sect of a uniquely Japanese strain of Buddhism, founded in the thirteenth century by Nichiren, a zealous monk who held that salvation could only be achieved through regular recitation of Lotus Sutra.

In the early 1960s Soka Gakkai began to spread outside Japan. The first international members were Japanese wives of American serviceman. In the late 1960s Soka Gakkai aimed specifically at recruiting non-Japanese Westerners by encouraging aggressive street proselytizing (much like Hare Krishna did during the same period), justifying it through the doctrine of *shakubuku*. In 1975 President Ikeda founded Soka Gakkai International (SGI) to coordinate the efforts of the various national Soka Gakkai organizations. The movement spread quickly and became the largest Buddhist group in the West, with particular strength in the U.S., Britain, Italy, and Brazil. (Today there are approximately 150,000 Soka Gakkai members in Brazil, with 60% of them of non-Japanese origin.) In 2005 the United States branch of SGI had 110,000 members, less than 15% of them Japanese-American. It is the only Buddhist group in the U.S. to have attracted a noticeable number of Hispanics and African-Americans.

SGI emphasizes individual choice and the need for self-responsibility, both highly valued American traits. It holds that individual practice is the first step towards world peace, and actively promotes this by engaging in international cultural and political projects. SGI's central practice of chanting the *daimoku* is both worldly, in that it promises material benefits (wealth and physical vitality) to devotees, and at the same time radical, in its emphasis on transforming the world. Soka Gakkai has given Nichiren Buddhism, the most evangelical and millennialist form of Buddhism in Japan, an international presence. Now, as a transnational religion concerned with global political and ethical issues, it remains an NRM worth watching.

NRMs that emphasize such personal transmission include Integral Yoga, founded by Swami Satchidananda (1914–2002) in 1966, and Siddha Yoga, founded by Swami Muktananda (1908–1982) who came to the U.S. in 1970.

The best known of the post-1965 Asian NRMs in the West is probably the International Society for Krishna Consciousness, abbreviated as **ISKCON**, and better known as Hare Krishna. The movement was founded by Swami Prabhupada (1896–1977). Prabhupada was an Indian businessman until he was initiated by a guru in 1933, and told to bring to the West the "Krishna consciousness," which can be traced to a sixteenth-century Bengali revival of a form of Hinduism devoted to the veneration of Krishna, an avatar of the deity Vishnu. Prabhupada arrived in 1965 in New York City and a year later founded the organization known as Hare Krishna.

Prabhupada quickly gathered a coterie of young Euro-Americans whom he taught to practice *sankirtana*, public singing and dancing in praise of Lord Krishna. To sing and dance in this manner was to practice *bhakti*, a Hindu term for following a path of loving devotion. This unconventional behavior, along with the male converts' shaved head with one long lock, gave the group some notoriety. By the mid-1970s, fifty ISKCON temples had been established throughout the United States, many with public vegetarian restaurants. The organization also established a presence in Europe, particularly in the U.K.

The late 1970s was the beginning of troubled times for ISKCON. Swami Prabhupada died without leaving a clear successor, and even before his death ISKCON's membership was in decline and its public image was tarnished. By the 1990s, leadership passed to a collective with the late Prabhupada chosen as the sole guru. Membership picked up as increasing numbers of South Asian immigrants to the West began to join, which has produced the unique situation of Euro-American gurus teaching South Asians.

Sikhism

Sikhism in the West has remained primarily an "ethnic religion" phenomenon with the notable exception of Sikh Dharma, formerly known as the 3HO Foundation or the Healthy, Happy, Holy Organization. The guru, Yogi Bhajan (1929–2004), arrived in the United States in 1969. In the U.S. he maintained his traditional Sikh identity but at the same time taught Kundalini yoga (physical exercises that awaken the energy latent at the base of the spine) to non-Sikhs, an act that estranged him from the ethnic Sikh community.

Sant Mat, a lineage of gurus associated with Sikhism, has been the guiding, if unacknowledged, force behind several NRMs. The Divine Light Mission was founded in India in the 1920s as an outreach movement of the Sant Mat tradition. At age eight, the son of the founder, known as Guru Maharaj Ji (1957–), became the spiritual leader. In 1971, the then fourteen-year-old "boy guru" came to the United States where the Divine Light Mission briefly became one of the fastest growing Asian-based NRMs in the West. Since 1983 called Élan Vital, the organization has dispensed with any Asian cultural trappings but retains its belief in the unity of all things and emphasis on the meetings known as *satsangs* (literally "the company of truth").

Eckankar is a New Religious Movement that also owes most of its ideas to the Sant Mat tradition (which it combines with Western esoteric traditions such Theosophy and Rosicrucianism). Eckankar was founded by Paul Twitchell (1908?–1971) in 1965. That year, he achieved divine realization and called himself the living Eck Master. Not only ideas but also whole paragraphs of Twitchell's writings are taken from the scriptures of a branch of Sant Mat. The aim of Eckankar is to become a "co-worker with God" through "the science of soul travel," which involves exploring different planes of reality. Eckankar teaches over one hundred different practices, many involving meditation based on light and sound. Teachings continue to evolve under the direction of the movement's leader (currently Harold Klemp), who is known as the living Eck Master.

In this chapter we will discuss new religions in China and Japan, with shorter sections on Korea and Vietnam. Leaving the West behind, we must revise what we learned earlier about new religions. Although our definition of NRMs as existing in tension with society holds strong for new religions in East Asia (as well as Africa and the Islamic world),  those outside the West do not face condemnation from the anticult movement in the same way as their Western counterparts. Neither do they arise from an esoteric counter-tradition, nor are they founded by gurus and masters from the other side of the world.

Like their Western counterparts, East Asian NRMs do have definable parent religions, but in East Asia any one NRM may have several parents. East Asian religions are by their very nature non-exclusive, and the region's NRMs are understandably eclectic, typically combining elements from indigenous shamanism, Buddhism, Daoism, local traditions, and sometimes Christianity. Most of all, though, East Asian NRMs draw from folk or popular religions but add membership commitments, charismatic leaders, and millennial expectations. Followers of East Asian NRMs also have a clear political agenda, which has sometimes brought them into conflict with the authorities. East Asian NRMs are not always overtly political, but they all advocate social reform. Finally, East Asians NRMs are experiential: believing is less important than practicing. Because these new religions do not hold to a distinction between body and spirit, they believe that physical exercises can cultivate the spirit and that good moral conduct can purify the body.

China

From prehistory to the early twentieth century

"New religions" have played an important role in Chinese history for thousands of years. China has a number of distinct features that have influenced how NRMs have been formed, and which have a bearing on how we can study them. China's centralized bureaucracy and culture of literacy have done a good job of keeping records of "dangerous cults" for the last two millennia. China's strong central authority has always been in tension with its regionalist tendencies. Until well into the twentieth century and the advent of mass communication and transport, much of the country was inaccessible from the imperial capital; it was via China's far-flung provinces that new ideas (such as Buddhism and Christianity) could enter from beyond the country's borders. It was from these geographic and political margins, too, that religious revolutionaries could proclaim new millennial kingdoms. China's long history has produced religious groups with characteristics that may seem surprisingly similar to the NRMs we find in the West, including charismatic leaders, millennial expectations, and an organized structure involving secrecy and initiation.

One of the earliest and best known of these groups is the "Yellow Turbans," which practiced Daoism combined with a veneration of local deities and charismatic healing. Their armed rebellion succeeded, and the Turbans operated as more or less an independent kingdom in eastern China from 140 C.E. until the ruling Han dynasty suppressed the movement and executed its leadership in 184. Named for their headgear, the Yellow Turbans followed a sacred scripture, the *Taiping Jing* ("Classic of the Great Peace"), which was the name of the millennial kingdom they hoped to usher in.

Succeeding dynasties would remember the lessons learned from the Yellow Turbans and be wary of fast-growing popular religious movements. The Tang dynasty (618–906 C.E.) saw China at the height of its political and cultural power, and its rulers patronized Daoist and Buddhist monasteries. After the Tang fell, the national religious establishment was weakened and local religious associations, pilgrimage sites, and worship centers grew in importance. This growth led to what scholars of Chinese history have called "sectarianism," but we may call New Religious Movements.

White Lotus groups began in the thirteenth century and spawned numerous sects through the end of the Qing dynasty (1644–1911).[1] White Lotus teachings had a Buddhist outlook, and in particular believed in the coming of Maitreya, the Buddha of the Future, who would offer salvation to followers. From popular Daoist cosmology, White Lotus borrowed the belief that the Eternal Ancient Mother was the creator of all. Most important, White Lotus groups operated as secret societies with apocalyptic and revolutionary aims.

In the fourteenth century, when Mongols ruled the country, the Red Turbans were a religio-political movement that combined not only Daoism and Buddhism but **Manicheanism**, an ancient Persian religion, which held to the view that the universe was locked in a struggle between the forces of light and dark. The Red Turbans associated themselves with a rebellion that successfully overthrew the Mongols. In 1368 one of the Red Turban leaders became known as Hung Wu, the first emperor of the new dynasty, which took the name Ming (light), a Manichean symbol. Ironically, one of Hung Wu's first acts as emperor was to outlaw all unorthodox religious groups. Still, these groups flourished underground for the next five hundred years.

When American and British missionaries began their evangelizing missions to China in the nineteenth century, Protestant Christianity was added to China's sectarian mix. One young man in rural south China, Hong Xiuquan (1814–1864), after learning about the Book of Revelation from a local missionary, had a vision of himself as Jesus' younger brother. Hong combined these millennial Protestant beliefs with visions of China as an agrarian Utopia (a common wish in Chinese religion and philosophy). Hong's growing following formed a military organization to protect against bandits, and recruited troops not only among believers but also from other armed peasant groups and secret societies. In 1851 Hong proclaimed the *Taiping Tianguo* or Heavenly Kingdom of Great Peace, a name that recalls the Yellow Turbans of some 1,800 years earlier and thus has great resonance in Chinese history. The aim of this new kingdom, with Hong himself as monarch, was to reconstitute a legendary ancient state based on egalitarian principles and cleansed of China's social ills, including arranged marriage, concubinage, opium smoking, and foot binding. The group's Protestant-inspired iconoclasm caused the Taiping revolutionaries to work towards the elimination of idol worship—and therefore to desecrate or destroy hundreds of Daoist and Buddhist temples.

The Taiping army took control of a swath of China, including the southern capital of Nanjing. But beset by internal feuding and corruption, the Heavenly Kingdom of Great Peace fell to the imperial army, helped by British and French forces. It is estimated that between the violent establishment of this millennial kingdom and its equally violent suppression, over thirty million lives were lost. The Taiping

Rebellion remains a testament to the impact that new religions can have on East Asian society.

The early twentieth century

The first half of the twentieth century was a time of unrivaled turmoil in China. The bitter end of the Qing dynasty in 1911, the subsequent drive towards modernization and Westernization (including campaigns against "superstition"), the Japanese invasion that began in 1931, and the civil wars between the Communists and Nationalists in the 1930s and 1940s, all took their toll on the religious establishment. Meanwhile, new religions proliferated. Many of these were related to the White Lotus societies, but scholars are only now uncovering their specific origins,

The largest family of new religions from this time is known as **Yiguandao**. Also spelled I-kuan-Tao, it translates as "the Way of Pervading Unity." Founded in the 1930s in eastern China, it is today popular in Taiwan and among overseas Chinese yet is still banned in mainland China. Although Yiguandao's international headquarters are in Los Angeles, the movement is almost completely unknown in the West. This is partly due to haziness over its exact origins and the fact that it seems to have evolved into several different lineage traditions, some of which do not refer to themselves as Yiguandao at all but rather by the more generic name Tian Dao ("the Way of Heaven").

The founder of the movement, Zhang Tianran (1889–1947), claimed to be the revealer of a secret tradition and the heir to an ancient lineage that includes the Buddha, the sixth-century B.C.E. philosopher Laozi, and many notables from Chinese history. Like the White Lotus groups, Yiguandao combines Buddhist millennialism, in the form of a belief in the coming of Maitreya, with popular Daoism, in the form of veneration of the Unborn Ancient Mother as the progenitor of all things. Yiguandao sees itself as the perfect combination of five religions: Buddhism, Daoism, Confucianism, Christianity, and Islam (five religions that were all active in early twentieth-century China).

The initiation ceremony of Yiguandao consists of three main rituals: the opening of the "secret pass" (or third eye) in the middle of the initiate's forehead, the giving of a secret handshake, and the teaching of a secret mantra. Once initiated, members of Yiguandao have few requirements (although vegetarianism is encouraged) yet feel a part of an international, semi-secret organization; this combination has made Yiguandao very appealing to Taiwanese businessmen, much like a Chinese version of Freemasonry. Yiguandao is currently the largest new religious movement in Taiwan, with several million initiates and several hundred thousand active members.

Religion in China today

On October 1, 1949, Chairman Mao Zedong of the Chinese Communist Party declared the founding the People's Republic of China. Since then the Communist Party has overseen all official political, cultural, and spiritual activities. Although the constitution officially allows for freedom of belief, religion in China has been tightly controlled by the Communist Party since its days as a guerrilla force. In the 1950s the party labeled Daoism and Buddhism feudal superstition, and Christianity foreign propaganda. It also rooted out and destroyed religious secret societies, including Yiguandao (which it accused, with some evidence, of collaborating with the Japanese invaders). These groups still flourish in Hong Kong, Taiwan, and Chinese communities around the world.

During the Cultural Revolution (1966–1976) all religion was proscribed (even as "the cult of Mao" became a religious force of tremendous power, complete with doctrines, rituals, and sacred texts). In the early 1980s some freedom of religion was reinstated and China began to experience a religious revival that as yet shows no sign of abating. Today there are five official religions in China: Daoism, Buddhism, Islam, Protestantism, and Catholicism. These are overseen at both national and local levels by the Religious Affairs Bureau. The clergy of each of these five traditions is salaried by the state.

Beyond officially sanctioned religious activity, many traditional practices take place in ethnic minority regions as well as in the countryside. By labeling these as folk customs, the government gives these practices implicit permission to continue. But any religious activity that is displeasing to the government might be labeled as *mixin* (superstition) or *xiejiao* (false sect, or cult), and thus forbidden.

Groups currently banned in China include not only Yiguandao but also many Christian movements. Before Protestant missionaries were expelled from China in 1949, they sowed the seeds for indigenous Chinese churches, many of which mixed popular practices, belief in a living savior, and New Testament apocalypticism. The largest of these congregational churches is the True Jesus Church, founded in 1917 in Beijing, the international headquarters of which are in Southern California and which has branches all over the Chinese Diaspora. The content and form of its religious services resemble mainstream Protestant institutions but with some notable differences: services, which are held on Saturdays, begin and end with a form of speaking in tongues, and sometimes include foot washing. A movement known as the Local Church, or more colloquially "The Shouters," founded by Chinese-born Watchman Nee (1903–1972) and Witness Lee (1905–1997) in the 1920s, also is now based in Southern California. Several offshoots of this movement have appeared in mainland China since the 1980s, with leaders proclaiming themselves the living Christ.

Related to these groups is the "house church" movement, unofficial groups of Chinese Christians meeting in private homes. Controversy exists over the nature and extent of this movement. Some have estimated that tens of millions of Chinese have attended these meetings at least once. Many house churches are simply Bible study groups formed by elderly Chinese, which the government allows to continue. Other house churches preach apocalyptic and **messianic** messages, and the government may find them potentially politically destabilizing.

NRMs and qigong

The most significant Chinese NRMs of the last fifty years are the qigong groups, which borrow doctrine from earlier sectarian groups and combine it with populist teaching and health culture. The word itself, which can be literally translated as breath-work or energy-skill, was coined in the twentieth century, but qigong's "self-cultivation" techniques—combining breathing, meditation, and calisthenics (bodily exercises)—have been a part of Chinese culture since records began. The word *qi* (pronounced "chee" and sometimes spelled "ch'i"), translated as breath, energy, or pneuma, is one of the basic concepts in Chinese cosmology. *Qi* is best defined as a pattern of bio-spiritual energy that circulates through the body along meridians—explicit but invisible pathways located in relationship to the body's organ systems.

Scholars believe that the origins of these self-cultivation practices, designed to increase and manage the flow of *qi*, may lie in the healing practices of ancient shamans. We know that as early as the fourth century B.C.E. breath training and gymnastics were practiced in China as forms of bio-spiritual cultivation, a means of achieving spiritual transcendence or even physical immortality. Ancient texts mention body cultivation among the techniques for attaining immortality.

All Chinese religious traditions engaged in body cultivation. Buddhism introduced yoga and specific meditation techniques from India, while the Confucian literati—the cultural elite who governed China—practiced "sitting in tranquility." But it was Daoism that maintained the most extensive repertoire of body cultivation practices, ranging from meditations through specific visualizations to "the inner alchemy" tradition, which sought to refine the elixir of immortality through the manipulation and combination of cosmic energies in the body. Later, body cultivation practices were a cornerstone of the combat techniques developed within the Buddhist and Daoist traditions of martial arts. (One of these traditions was the series of slow, continuous movements known as tai chi—"Supreme Ultimate"—today practiced by millions around the world.) And of course, the White Lotus groups used a variety of body cultivation methods, including healing techniques and martial arts, to recruit new members.

One body cultivation movement active in northern China between 1899 and 1901 believed that their particular form of martial arts could confer invincibility against Western military technology. This group was known as the "Fists of Righteousness and Harmony," or in English as the Boxers. The Boxer Rebellion of 1900 was the second most powerful internal political challenge to the collapsing Qing dynasty, after Hong Xiuquan's Kingdom of Great Peace.

In the 1950s, even as the Communists were stamping out all secret societies and religious lineages that practiced body cultivation, they were standardizing and secularizing these same techniques and developing a series of clinics where qigong was taught as a form of physical therapy. All official qigong activity stopped during the Cultural Revolution, but from the mid-1970s the government sponsored research into "qigong science," which often focused on the paranormal abilities that qigong practitioners could develop. (Known in Chinese as "extraordinary functions," these abilities included telekinesis, clairvoyance, and extrasensory perception or ESP.) Qigong practitioners claimed that they could cure disease by transmitting their qi to others externally. As the scientific establishment began increasingly to question the results of these experiments, enthusiasm for qigong among ordinary Chinese people started to take on the qualities of a religious revival.

CLOSE-UP

Falun Gong

The largest and best known of the qigong movements is also one of the youngest, founded in 1992 by Li Hongzhi. Li lived in the economically depressed northeastern city of Changchun, when he began to teach publicly a new form of qigong which he claimed to be ancient (a common feature of Chinese NRMs, as we have seen). This he called Falun Dafa, the Great Law of the Dharma Wheel, although it was better known as Falun gong (Dharma Wheel skill).

Falun gong began as a qigong network like the others. By this time, most of the other qigong movements of the "qigong fever" period were losing popularity, so Falun gong picked up former practitioners with its stripped down qigong routine concentrating on five exercises. In 1994, Li expounded a more explicitly religious message, with a promise of salvation for all who practice Falun gong. The concept of "Fa" was revealed to be the Great Law, or Dharma, of the universe. Li's speeches were collected and published, and the resulting text, *Zhuan Falun* ("Turning the Dharma Wheel"), became the movement's sacred scripture, itself seen to be saturated with Fa. Falun gong practitioners were forbidden to learn about or practice any other qigong or religious system.

Practicing Falun gong was not just a matter of doing the five qigong exercises, but of cultivating one's *xinxing* (spiritual nature) through trials in daily life. According to the *Zhuan Falun*, the suffering experienced by Falun gong members would cultivate their natures and transform their bodies. Master Li could also aid personally (though not necessarily in person) in members' transformation by psychically inserting a Falun or "dharma wheel" into their bodies.

Within the first four years of its existence, Falun gong grew to between ten and twenty million adherents (nobody knew the exact number) through its active proselytizing and its emphasis on morality and discipline, appearing to many as the antidote to a corrupt one-party system and the rampant materialism of Communist China. In 1996 Falun gong became more political. Whenever a government official or journalist criticized the group publicly, mass protests—including letter-writing campaigns and sit-ins—would be mobilized. In early 1999, for example, a dozen Falun gong leaders were arrested at a public demonstration against a local magazine that had published a negative story on the group. Falun gong responded to these arrests with its largest demonstration yet: in April 1999, ten thousand members protested peacefully outside Zhongnanhai, the residential compound for China's top leaders, adjacent to Tiananmen Square in Beijing, deliberately striking at the heart of the Chinese party and state. In July the party and state struck back: Falun gong was declared a *xiejiao*, an evil cult, and its practice was made illegal. Chinese television aired round-the-clock anti-Falun gong propaganda. Members were put in jail indefinitely unless they renounced their faith, and were often tortured.

Meanwhile Li Hongzhi had moved to the United States and Falun gong has spread around the world, both among Chinese and others. In the West, Falun gong has mutated yet again, this time into a political organization that sends practitioners to participate in twenty-four-hour protest vigils in front of all Chinese embassies and consulates, and collects approving proclamations from Western governments.

Publicly, Falun gong uses the discourse of human rights to attack the Chinese state and the ruling Com-

Falun gong members reading the words of the religion's founder, Li Hongzhi. In the background posters display Falun gong's symbol, which combines the Buddhist swastika, the Daoist yin–yang, and the Chinese words for "Truthfulness, Benevolence, and Forbearance."

munist Party, in particular Jiang Zemin, the former leader of both. (Falun gong's more internally directed literature sees an apocalyptic showdown between itself and the Communist Party.) Meanwhile, the Chinese government uses anticult rhetoric to justify its continued suppression of the movement in China. As David Palmer, a foremost scholar of Falun gong, put it:

> Today, the Communist Party and Falun gong continue to wage a propaganda war before world public opinion, a war that draws heavily on gory images of mutilated bodies. Official Chinese sources show images of alleged Falun gong practitioners who, for instance, set themselves on fire or cut open their bellies to pull out the rotating swastika planted by the master. Falun gong literature and websites provide photographic documentation of the scarred and burnt body parts of tortured practitioners.[2]

Falun gong is an NRM that did not exist fifteen years ago yet which at its peak probably had more practitioners than there are Jews or Sikhs in the world. It has also offered the most sustained challenge the Communist Party of China has faced over the last fifty years. In other words, despite the fact that it is not fully understood in the West, Falun gong may be the most significant NRM active today.

In the late 1980s, China experienced what became widely known as "qigong fever." Charismatic qigong masters, claiming to be heirs to ancient lineages of secret transmission, would fill sixty-thousand-seater sports stadiums with qigong meetings in which participants were healed or went into trance. These "force-filled lectures" soon attracted the notice of the government, which realized that in promoting qigong as a new Chinese science and medicine it had created a Frankenstein's monster that it could not control. The authorities "invited" the qigong master Yan Xin to leave China and never return. He and many other qigong masters have settled overseas and found a niche in New Age and alternative medicine circles, adding to the growing interest in the West for Asian religions. The anti-qigong movement culminated in the government crackdown on Falun gong, a movement that is looked at in detail in the Close-up feature (p. 72).

Modern qigong movements share common themes with other East Asian new religions, past and present, viewing the universe as a living entity made up of unseen but controllable forces. The messianic apocalypticism seen in many Chinese religious movements from the Yellow Turbans on is also present in later qigong groups. Qigong masters are more than just healers or physical trainers; they are moral redeemers, who offer salvation at a biological as well as a spiritual level. Qigong groups are also nationalist: just as previous Chinese groups aimed to overthrow foreign dynasties or Western colonial powers, so too do qigong groups want to put an end to Western scientific superiority.

Vietnam

Vietnam was occupied by China for the first thousand or so years C.E., and thus its religious life has been dominated by China's three teachings: Buddhism, Daoism, and Confucianism. When the French began to colonize Vietnam in the mid-nineteenth century they brought with them not only Catholicism, but also a popular French religion known as "**Spiritism.**" Similar to the American NRM Spiritualism, Spiritism was founded in 1857 by Allan Kardec (1804–1869) and promoted an interest in séances to contact the spirit world. This interest, combined with a revitalization of the Daoist folk tradition of spirit writing, gave birth to Vietnam's best-known NRM, Cao Dai.

People assemble to worship at Cao Dai's Great Temple near Saigon, Vietnam. Known as "The Holy See," Cao Dai's headquarters is one of the largest religious complexes in Southeast Asia.

The founder, Ngo Van Chieu (1878–1932?), was an official of the French colonial administration who took a great interest in Kardec's Spiritism. In 1920 he was contacted by a divinity named Cao Dai ("high platform" in Chinese) and in 1926 he and two fellow diviners promulgated the document known as "The Declaration of the Founding of the Cao Dai Religion." Through séances and spirit writing, the leaders of Cao Dai contacted an extremely eclectic pantheon including Laozi, Confucius, the Buddha, Jesus, and various Western literary figures, most famously Victor Hugo. Despite its condemnation by the French administration and the Buddhist establishment, Cao Dai is believed to have attracted around half a million followers within the first few years of its founding. Cao Dai sees itself as the unification of Asian and Western traditions, and expects to play a part in the coming political and religious revolution. These expectations resulted in the creation of an independent army that shifted its alliances to suit its nationalist aims: after allying with the Japanese in ejecting the French, it fought alongside the Vietminh (Ho Chi Minh's revolutionary army)—again against the French—and finally turned against the Vietminh. The Communist Party of Vietnam, like its counterpart in China, tolerates no competition and stripped Cao Dai of its businesses, its land, and most of its priesthood.

Cao Dai's headquarters, known as the "The Holy See," lies in a city northwest of Saigon (Ho Chi Minh City), but the Vietnamese expatriate community in Australia and North America has become the movement's de facto political and financial driving force.

Cao Dai has much in common with Chinese NRMs. Like the Taiping Rebellion, it fielded a powerful army. It arose around the same time as Yiguandao and under some of the same turbulent circumstances; it also is an evangelical and eclectic faith.

Korea

Like Vietnam, Korea has been under China's influence since the first century C.E., though more as a tributary than as a conquest. Koreans adapted the "Three Teachings" of Chinese religious traditions (Buddhism, Daoism, Confucianism) while retaining their indigenous shamanic culture. The first known Korean NRMs developed in the late nineteenth century out of the same matrix that we saw in China (peasant rebellions and social instability) at the same time as Western culture, technology, and religion were beginning to undermine Korean culture. Indeed, Korea was the Asian country most affected by Protestant missionaries. A response was the Donghak (Eastern learning) Rebellion of 1894, a name taken to show Korean opposition to Sohak (Western learning). Like the Taipings and Boxers, Donghak was a political movement inspired by a religious awakening. Donghak combined elements from the Three Teachings with an underlying Korean shamanism. Like its East Asian counterparts, millennial expectations of a New Age led Donghak leaders to marshal an army. The Donghak Rebellion lasted about a year, at the end of which its leaders were executed.

Out of the ashes of the Donghak Rebellion came several New Religious Movements. The best known of these is Cheondogyo, founded in 1860, which in 2005 had more than a million members. Its worship centers on Hanulnim, the Lord of Heaven, a god indigenous to Korea and therefore not foreign like Buddhist and Christian gods. The Cheondogyo movement was originally strongest in the north of the country, but under the autocratic regime of the present Democratic Republic of Korea (North Korea) its status is uncertain.

JeungSanDo is another combinatory religion that emerged out of the Donghak Rebellion. It was founded by SangJeNim (1871–1909), who claimed to be the latest incarnation of God (previous incarnations included the Jade Emperor, Maitreya, and Jesus Christ). Worship involves chanting a mantra while performing a set of sixteen tai chi movements. JeungSanDo's sacred scripture was published in English in 1995, which facilitated the international spread of this religion.

The best-known Korean NRM has already been discussed in Chapter 2: the Unification Church, founded by Sun Myung Moon in 1954. Like other Korean NRMs it is **syncretistic**, shamanistic, and nationalistic. Perhaps the fastest growing Korean NRM today, however, is DahnHak, which means "Vitality Learning." Founded in Seoul in 1985, DahnHak teaches a standardized five-step program to increase the circulation of the *qi* through the body's internal channels, promoting physical health, with the promise that regular practitioners will also attain spiritual enlightenment and contribute towards the creation of world peace. As such DahnHak resembles nothing so much as a Chinese qigong group. In 1994 Dr. Ilchi Lee, the founder of Dahn-Hak, moved to the U.S. where, under the name of the Healing Society, the movement has been growing steadily. It has received some negative press about the extreme training procedures at its more advanced levels of practice, in particular after a woman died of heat exhaustion during a DahnHak training session in the Arizona Desert.

Japan

Japanese New Religious Movements, at least compared to their East Asian counterparts, have been well studied by Western scholars. Any decent university library will own several standard English language books about Japanese NRMs, mostly written by Westerners living in Japan in the 1950s and 1960s. These scholars must have found it fascinating to discover and write about these NRMs with their apparently unlikely founders (many of whom were female), their belief in magical powers, their unique doctrines, and their baroque rituals. They must also have found Japanese NRMs relatively easy to study: unlike Shinto and Buddhism, which were so tightly woven both into each other and into the political and social fabric of Japan that they could be difficult to disentangle, these new religions seemed to Western eyes to have a clear "religious" identity. They had founders, sacred texts, readily articulated doctrines, and centers of worship. In post-war Japan there were so many NRMs that one Western scholar titled his book on the subject "The Rush Hour of the Gods." Overall, it has been estimated that one-fourth of Japanese have at least a casual involvement with NRMs, making Japan the society most impacted by NRMs.

Japanese NRMs, although derived from a variety of Buddhist or Shinto traditions and originating in different social and geographical locations, and varying in size from a few hundred to millions of followers, share many common traits. Most were founded by strong, charismatic, and divinely inspired laypeople, often with shamanic or mediumistic power. The founders are often known as *ikigami* (a living *kami*: one possessed by deity), which are seen as persons filled with power—not necessarily living gods or messiahs. The founders are disproportionately women, which is notable in such a male-centered society. Both male and female founders have told their personal stories of how they overcame adversity; thus they are models, not just leaders, for their followers. When these founders die, leadership is often passed through their children.

Japanese NRMs are propagated through lay members rather than the monks and priests of Buddhism or Shinto. NRM members become part of a highly centralized organization, with a headquarters that houses administration buildings, the main temple, guesthouses for pilgrims, and theological training schools.

Unlike other East Asian NRMs we have seen, most Japanese NRMs are not overtly political and revolutionary, but instead call for spiritual transformation of the world. But Japanese NRMs are similar to their East Asian cousins in their emphasis on personal experience. Most focus on individual spiritual cleansing and healing to eliminate bad karma. Japanese NRMs share a correlative worldview, which Helen Hardacre, a scholar of Japanese religion, sums up as seeing "individual, society, nature, and the universe as an integrated system vitalized by a single principle."[3] Religious practice thus consists of integration of the self with the physical, social, and spiritual bodies.

The history of Japanese NRMs

Japanese NRMs spread so quickly, are so prevalent, and hold such a broad appeal that their role is akin to that of non-denominational Protestant churches in the West. Why is this so? It is tempting to explain the proliferation of Japanese NRMs as a reaction to a social crisis in Japan, though making this the sole reason would be reductionist. What is irrefutable is that over the last two hundred years Japan has undergone immense social change, as the country has been transformed from one of the world's most tradition-based feudal societies to one of its most modern.

Scholars often see Japanese NRMs as breaking into four waves. The first, from 1800 to 1860, coincided with the declining years of the Tokugawa shogunate and the forced opening of Japan to the West. Some Japanese peasants may have reacted to worsening political and economic conditions by turning towards rural shamans whose revealed texts promised hope and renewal. Under these conditions arose the earliest Japanese NRMs: **Kurozumikyo**, Tenrikyo, and Konkokyo.

Tenrikyo, the Religion of Heavenly Wisdom, is still one of the largest and most important Japanese NRMs. It was founded in 1838 by Nakayama Miki (1798–1887), who in summoning various deities to cure her son's illness found herself possessed by *kami* and became, in effect, a living shrine. While possessed, Nakayama wrote the Ofudesaki, the sacred text, which instructs how to "polish" the self, removing "spiritual dust." Nakayama also revealed that her hometown was the Jiba, the place of humankind's origins and where God the Parent resides. A sacred pillar, known as the Kanrodai, marks that spot and continues to be the center of pilgrimage. Seeing her mission as delivering people from suffering, Nakayama began to propagate this new religion, though her activity was repeatedly suppressed at first. Nonetheless, Tenrikyo spread throughout Japan, and in 2005 the group had three million members worldwide.

Where Tenrikyo spread because of its promise of realization of the ideal world, Konkokyo prospered because of its emphasis on the present world and human principles. It was founded in 1859 by the farmer Kawate Bunjiro (1814–1883). After an illness, Kawate had an encounter with Konjin, a malevolent spirit. Kawate realized this fearsome demon was in fact the God of All The Universe. At first, Kawate taught farmers the true nature of Konjin. Later, though, the deity occupied Kawate's body and Kawate proclaimed himself a living *kami*, known as Konko Daijin, "the Great Kami of Golden Light."

The current religious leader of Konkokyo is Konko Daijin V, a direct male descendent of the founder. The leader acts as mediator between various *kami* and members, ensuring their health and prosperity. Konkokyo today has about 400,000 followers, with about 1,600 churches in Japan and another twenty around the world.

The second wave of Japanese NRMs occurred in the 1920s and 1930s amidst growing urbanization and economic depression. The general failure of established Buddhism and Shinto to put across their message in accessible terms allowed NRMs to thrive in new urban communities. Even Tenrikyo and the other "older" NRMs, which had begun in rural areas, now found their strength in the cities. In particular, a number of popular Buddhist-inspired lay movements flourished. Nichiren Buddhism, the most evangelistic, uncompromising, and materialist of all Buddhist sects, seemed to have enjoyed special resonance in this period, as it gave birth to not only Reiyukai and its offshoot, Rissho Koseikai—which today is the second largest Japanese NRM—but also to Soka Gakkai, discussed in the previous chapter. The 1920s and 1930s also saw the rise of Fascist government, which crushed any religion that could potentially challenge its authority, so NRMs in this second wave were often mercilessly persecuted (unlike those in the first wave, which often cooperated with the government). Soka Gakkai opposed official State Shinto, and its leaders were jailed during World War II. The founder, Tsuesaburo Makiguchi (1871–1944), died in prison, while his aide, Josei Toda (1900–1958), survived to become the next president.

The third wave of NRMs took place against the backdrop of post-war reconstruction. On December 15, 1945, an American army colonel signed the Directive for the Disestablishment of State Shinto. In order to "prevent a recurrence of the perversion of Shinto theory and beliefs into militaristic and ultra-nationalistic propaganda," the Allied Command forced a separation between the Shinto religion and the government, while protecting independent religions against persecution by the state.[4] This "American-style" religious freedom gave rise to a host of NRMs. By the early 1950s, Western observers reported six hundred new religions in Japan. Older NRMs that had been persecuted during the war years because they opposed Japanese expansionism came out of hiding and increased their membership. Still other NRMs, which had cooperated with the wartime government, reconstituted themselves as peace-loving groups. All appealed to a Japanese society that lay in ruins, sometimes quite literally. New groups were formed in Japan every year, a situation that continues to this day. All had to register with the state, but otherwise remained free of government control.

The sheer number of Japanese NRMs in the post-war period has meant that many of them have become known in Japan by a single distinguishing characteristic—which has not always been the most relevant one. For example, Tensho Kotai Jingukyo (the Religion of the Universe's Ultimate God), founded in 1945, is nicknamed "the Dancing Religion" because of its monthly ceremony involving rhythmic movements. Perfect Liberty Kyodan, founded in 1946, was known as "the Golf Religion" because its headquarters included several golf courses at a time when golf was a growing passion (and an exorbitant luxury) among Japanese businessmen. In fact, P.L. Kyodan's most important tenet is that life is art, and thus the movement emphasizes traditional Japanese arts such as flower arranging and archery, far more than golfing. Makuya, founded in 1948, is one of the few Japanese NRMs to be derived from Christianity. It is best known for its closeness with the state of Israel, the existence of which the religion believes must be supported to fulfill biblical prophecy. Many members volunteer in Israel or at least tour the country. Despite their peculiarities, the "dancing," "golf," and "Israel" religions, along with most other NRMs in Japan, share similar basic values and practices.

Japanese NRMs had outposts among Japanese communities abroad from the early twentieth century on. But beginning in the 1960s, some NRMs began to proselytize to non-Japanese. Many Japanese NRMs are distinguished by their missionary zeal, unlike traditional Japanese religion, which has no interest in converting non-Japanese. Today, Japanese NRMs are found in eighty countries, most prominently the United States (particularly the West Coast and Hawaii), Brazil, and Korea. Still, except for Soka Gakkai, none has had notable success gaining converts among non-Japanese. Scholars have accounted for this failure by noting that Japanese NRMs are rooted in Japanese culture, including ideas about *kami* and ancestors, as well as nationalism: many view Japan itself as sacred.

The fourth wave of NRMs in Japan began in the 1970s and 1980s. Movements in this wave are often referred to as *shin shin shukyo* ("new new religions"). These groups gained members quickly through active and brash conversion techniques. Their worldview was more magical and millennialist than that of earlier Japanese NRMs: adherents expected miraculous interventions and performed exorcisms. Mahikari is a prominent example. Although formed in 1959, it rose to prominence in the 1970s and is known for its distribution of magical amulets and its central ritual of one believer using "spirit rays" to cast out evil from another believer's body.

The growth of these fourth-wave NRMs was aided by the con-comitant rise of a general "esoteric milieu." Since the mid-1970s Japanese bookstores have been well stocked with volumes about aliens, "histories" of the lost continents of Mu and Atlantis, tales of spirit pos-session, and guides to the "power of positive thinking." (China has also seen this kind of publishing boom, but only since the late 1990s.) Although this growing interest in alternative spiritualities owes some-thing to international New Age culture, it also can be read as a latest incarnation of a deep source of East Asian culture: a belief in a living world inhabited by personal spiritual powers.

The latest phase in the history of Japanese NRMs began in 1995, when members of Aum Shinrikyo released poison gas into the Tokyo subway (see Chapter 1). Before then, although the press reg-ularly accused NRMs (and other religious organizations) of financial misdeeds, civil authorities rarely responded to these accusations. But the government's mass arrests and raids of Aum were fully supported by the Japanese public. The Aum subway massacre led to a general anti-NRM backlash in Japan, with American "anticult" experts traveling to the country to lecture on how cults brainwash their converts and pose a menace to society. There has been public debate over which NRM will be "the next Aum," with Soka Gakkai the leading contender, despite its proclaimed message of peace. There has also been increased hostility towards non-Japanese NRMs, especially the Unification Church. Still, legal protections do exist, and this phase is best seen as another chapter in this history of Japanese NRMs rather than the end of the story.

This chapter considers the staggering number and variety of religious movements that have formed over the last two hundred years in sub-Saharan (Black) Africa and in the Black Diaspora. Only a few of the most significant will be described specifically here.

Sub-Saharan Africa has over six hundred million people divided into two thousand ethnic groups, who speak seven hundred indigenous languages.

The continent is immensely diverse, as are the new religions it has produced. But many of them share common features. One reason for this is that African New Religious Movements developed out of a common factor that was not at all of African making, namely European domination. Beginning in the middle of the fifteenth century, European nations began to enslave and export African slaves, a process which did not end until the late nineteenth century. At the same time Europeans began to establish trading posts along the African coast, and beginning in the eighteenth century, began to explore and colonize the interior. Between 1880 and 1912 all of sub-Saharan Africa apart from Ethiopia fell under European control. These two processes, the international slave trade and colonization, put Africans in sudden, unwanted contact with European Christianity and Western values and lifestyle. If slavery and colonization were African "problems," then one way in which Africa solved these problems creatively was through developing new religions.

Another reason for common features of African NRMs is that they all owe something to traditional African religions. These are oral traditions with few texts to their name, which have, over the centuries, been influenced by the spread of Christianity and Islam (which has grown piecemeal in Africa since the seventh century) as well as by intertribal relations. As a result, reconstructing ancient or "original" African customs is largely guesswork. Despite these difficulties, we know that most African tribes were polytheist, worshipping many gods, but also believed in (but did not directly worship) a high god who created the world but withdrew from it and is no longer directly concerned with its affairs. A pantheon of lesser deities, often representing the forces of nature, is more interested in humanity and requires a reciprocal relationship with it based on sacrifice, divination, and possession. Tribal ancestors also participate in human affairs. These deities and ancestors do not offer the promise of a heavenly afterlife, as in some other religions, but are highly active in the daily life of those who worship them.

In traditional African religions, spiritual authority figures serve to link the human and the divine worlds. These men or women may function as monarchs, priests, diviners, prophets, or all of the above. The role of the prophet as revolutionary leader has become particularly important to African NRMs, perhaps because of the influence of Islam and Christianity, both of which have traditions of prophetic social criticism. As Christianity has penetrated further into Africa over the last hundred years, some elements of traditional religion have weakened or disappeared altogether. For example, many of the local pantheons are now extinct or have been interpreted, from a Christian perspective, as demonic. Other aspects have endured, however. As we will see, spirit possession religions, in which supplicants may receive advice, cure, comfort, or reprimands for their wrongdoings from deities speaking through entranced mediums, have flourished in particular.

African Neo-Traditional NRMs

Neo-traditional NRMs is the name given to religions that reconfigure certain aspects of traditional African life in the face of modernity. Most of these neo-traditional NRMs take the form of possession religions. Two of the best known are the religions of the Bori and the Zar. These names refer to groupings of individually named spirits. While some of these spirits are beneficial, others can cause illness. Belief in these spirits flourishes in countries such as Niger and Sudan, where Islam is the official religion but where, at the same time, traditional practices are maintained by much of the population. Adherents of the Bori or Zar religions—the exact number of which is unknown—are mainly poor women who feel a measure of religious and social power from interacting with these sprits. For these devotees, Bori and Zar coexist with Islam, even though the dominant Islamic theology considers the Bori and Zar to be evil spirits.

Perhaps the best known African neo-traditional spirit possession religion is the Hauka, which was widespread in West Africa from the 1920s to the 1950s. The Hauka "cult" became notorious after it was the subject of a famous documentary film, *Les Maîtres Fous* ("The Mad Masters"), made by Jean Rouch (1917–2004) in 1953.

Hauka participants were usually rural migrants of Songhay ethnicity who came to cities such as Accra in Ghana (then the Gold Coast, a British colony), where they found work as laborers. They entered a trance and were possessed by various spirits associated with the Western colonial powers. Like many other possession religions, the Hauka sect coexisted with Islam and incorporated many Islamic saints and heroes into its rituals. Most of its adherents were Muslims.

The film *Les Maîtres Fous* shows a Hauka group ritual at a farm outside Accra. After they finish their work as laborers, men gather and put on costumes to represent the governor general, the English doctor and his wife, the commander of the military garrison, and other notables. The film's disturbing images are powerful—men foaming at the mouth, and sacrificing and eating a dog—but equally powerful is the implicit indictment of colonialism. After Ghana achieved its independence, the Hauka cult subsided, reabsorbed into traditional possession religions that did not incorporate colonial figures.

African Initiated Churches

The number of adherents of neo-traditional movements is minuscule compared to those who follow African NRMs based on Christianity—churches founded by Africans for Africans, often in response to Protestant missionary work. These are usually called African Initiated Churches (abbreviated as AICs: the "I" can also stand for Independent, Indigenous, or Instituted).

Christianity in Africa: background

Although AICs can rightly be considered NRMs, it does not follow that Christianity should be considered a new or alternative religion in Africa. In fact, for the first five hundred years, at least, of the Christian Church, Africa was its geographic center entirely. The two earliest nations where the government proclaimed Christianity as the state religion were African. Despite two millennia of change, these national churches still exist today as the Ethiopian Orthodox and Egyptian Coptic churches.

Until recently most inhabitants of sub-Saharan Africa practiced either traditional religions or Islam, which is still growing rapidly and presently has 130 million adherents in the region. Christianity made its reappearance in Africa in the sixteenth and seventeenth centuries in the form of Catholic missionaries, who successfully converted the King of the Kongo (a kingdom in central Africa). Protestant missions of the nineteenth and twentieth centuries spread even further on the vanguard of European colonialism. With the decolonization of Africa in the 1950s and 1960s, some predicted that African Christianity would decline. In fact, the opposite has been the case. In 1965, 25% of all sub-Saharan Africans were Christian and today the figure is approximately 46%, or almost 300 million people. Africans are converting to Christianity at the rate of 8.4 million a year. Most African Christians are Catholic, Anglican, or Methodist, but AICs have also enjoyed significant growth, and it is to them that we now turn.

The development of AICs

The earliest AICs date from the end of the nineteenth century and often had the word "Ethiopian" or "African" as part of their name. Churches called themselves "Ethiopian" not because the leaders or members were from Ethiopia (most began in South Africa) but because Ethiopia was the first Christian nation and represented a definitively African Christianity. These churches were modeled on their European counterparts and formed in order to gain independence from the White mission churches. They have been in decline for the last fifty years, caught as they are between the large international Christian denominations and the "prophet healing" AICs.

Most AICs fall into a category that is sometimes called "Prophet-healing" or "Spiritual." They emphasize the power of the Holy Spirit and are often founded by prophets who see themselves as divinely appointed and who lead on the basis of dreams and visions. Their followers might take these prophets as a substitute for or equal to Christ. An example is Simon Kimbangu, founder of the largest African Initiated Church. An account of the beginning of Kimbangu's ministry relates that "because Simon Kimbangu obeyed the voice of Jesus, all things promised by Jesus were fulfilled in him, the work of Jesus was revealed, and the names of God the father and of the Lord Jesus were glorified."[1] Claims such as this led some Western theologians to accuse AICs of not being truly Christian. These prophetic leaders were often arrested, exiled, or killed by colonial authorities, and their martyrdom strengthened their budding churches. While political oppression led to messianic expectations, after decolonization many of these AICs became almost mainstream, settling into highly institutionalized organizations in which the founder's powers seem ever more legendary.

Some of these Prophet-healing AICs resemble Pentecostalism, the offshoot of Protestantism founded in the United States at the beginning of the twentieth century, which emphasizes speaking in tongues and miraculous healings as the workings of the Holy Spirit. Their differences, however, are important: the distinctive dress of the leadership, the use of symbolic power objects (called fetishes in English) for healing rituals, and the dietary and other prohibitions distinguish them from the worldwide Pentecostal movement. The largest Prophet-healing AICs include the South African-based Nazareth Baptist Church, founded by the Zulu prophet Isaiah Shembe (1870–1935) in 1911; the Aladura Churches, related denominations strong in West Africa; and the Kimbanguist Church from Central Africa, which will be discussed in the Close-up feature (p. 92). All of these groups have memberships in the millions.

The newest group of AICs is called Pentecostal or **Charismatic**; they are a part of the international non-denominational congregations that have been growing steadily worldwide since the 1970s. Compared with earlier movements these AICs are much less accepting of traditional African values; for example, their healing ceremonies use the laying on of hands rather than power objects. These churches appeal to Africa's new urban class and tend to preach a gospel of material prosperity. They are particularly strong in West Africa. Among the best known is The Deeper Life Bible Church of Nigeria. Founded in 1982, it had half a million members in 2005. Its main church has the largest congregation in Lagos.

Understanding AICs

How Christian are the Prophet-healing AICs? From the perspective of some Western Christians, AICs cannot be accepted as Christian, but instead represent a reversion to primitive "animism" or "heathenism" (European terms for traditional African religion) under the guise of Christianity. To phrase the same argument in a way that is less hostile to traditional religion, one might say that Africans never really converted to European Christianity at all; rather, the European missionaries' ethnocentric and condescending attitude kept them from forging a deep connection with the Africans to whom they were supposedly teaching the Gospel. The AICs only pay lip service to European norms. Evidence to support these views includes AICs' use of fetishes, their continued practice of polygamy, and their sacralization of African lands.

The above critiques suggest that AICs are tribal religions with a veneer of Christianity. They are, however, quite different from traditional non-literate tribal religions, which lack two features that AICs exhibit quite strongly: a missionary impulse and a conception of salvation in the next life. Moreover, AICs place great importance on the written word, namely the Bible. Of course, as is the case everywhere, Africans have developed their own interpretation of the Holy Book. Many AICs were founded on a conviction that missionaries had neglected to teach them the "real" Bible, or had deliberately concealed its true meaning. At the very least, missionaries ignored some of the Bible's powerful implications. The importance of ancestors, purity laws, and the struggle for national liberation were seen by Africans as crucial themes in the Hebrew Scriptures that were disregarded by the missionaries.

In responding to specifically African needs, AICs have grown phenomenally, from 42,000 members in 1900 to 83 million members in 2000. This growth comes despite the persecution of AICs in the early twentieth century by colonial governments and mission churches. In Southern, Central, and Western Africa, a large proportion of the population follows these NRMs. Indeed, 44% of the population of Southern Africa is said to belong to an AIC.

AICs are growing outside of Africa as well, becoming truly global NRMs. They first appeared in the U.K. in the 1920s, and by the 1960s the Aladura and other West African AICs had a large presence there. As African immigration into Europe swelled in the 1980s and 1990s, increasing numbers of AICs—especially of the Pentecostal/Charismatic variety—opened outposts there, in particular in Germany and France. Although these AICs abroad function mainly as ethnic churches, they do have some White members and many see secularized Europe as a mission field, reversing commonly held ideas of who missionizes to whom.

NRMs of the African Diaspora

Afro-Catholic NRMs

From the beginning of the Atlantic slave trade in the late fifteenth century until Brazil abolished slavery in 1888, some ten to twelve million Africans made the "middle passage" to the New World, where they were sold as slaves. Of these, only about two million came to North America. The rest were sent to South America or the Caribbean. These slaves were strongly influenced by Catholicism, which they often combined with traditional West African religion to form distinctively new religious traditions. These include Vodou in Haiti, Santeria in Cuba, and Candomble in Brazil. In all of these traditions, worship focuses on a pantheon of spirits with human attributes (called *lwa* in Vodou and *orisha* in Santeria and Candomble) who mediate between the mundane world and the creator god. As each spirit is also identified with a particular Catholic saint, practitioners can be both devout Catholics and "servants" of the spirits. Spirits mediate through divination, sacrifice, or trance. Initiates of these religions can be possessed (or "ridden") by the spirit of which they are particular devotees. These religions might be best understood as a network of relationships between humans, ancestors, African spirits, and Catholic saints.

The word Vodou was first used in 1797 to describe a ceremonial dance performed by slaves in Haiti, a French colony. The description came from a French traveler who warned of its revolutionary potential. When a successful slave revolt gave Haiti independence in 1804, the new Black rulers proclaimed Catholicism the official religion (which it remains today). Throughout the nineteenth century, however, the Catholic Church refused to send priests to Haiti, and Vodou became the effective faith of all but the most elite Haitians. Despite the Church's subsequent violent "anti-superstition" campaigns (in 1896, 1913, and 1941), as well as the Haitian dictator "Papa Doc" Duvalier's use of Vodou, Vodou is today recognized as a source of national pride and culture. It is practiced not only in Haiti but also in the large Haitian communities of Miami, New York, Boston, and Montreal, making Vodou a new religion in the West.

By the early nineteenth century, Cuban society was a maze of classes, castes, and racial and ethnic groups. Creoles—Cubans of mixed African and European descent—joined formal clubs (called *cabildos*) which, though sanctioned by the Roman Catholic Church, in fact promoted the traditional religion of the Yoruba, the ethnic group of many African slaves. During carnival dances, each *cabildo* would embody a particular god in the guise of a saint. From these origins came the religions known as the Way of the Saints, Santeria. Cubans of all walks of life might consult *santeros* (initiated Santeria masters) on a fee-for-service basis. A *santero* must learn how to be ridden by the spirit; this is called becoming an *asiento* (seat). The first step is a year-long novitiate, which is known as *iyawo* (bride of *orisha*). An *iyawo* is subject to many restrictions before becoming a full *santero*. Such apprenticeship requires financial and personal commitment.

Santeria was revived during the afro-cubanismo cultural movement of the 1940s and 1950s, and the Cuban Diaspora has further strengthened the religion. Botanicas (shops that provide candles, statues, and other Santerian accoutrements) are now familiar sights in North American cities and online.

In the Brazilian city of Bahia, Yoruba people were in the majority. In the early nineteenth century, free Africans and emancipated slaves combined not only Yoruba and Catholic but also indigenous Amerindian beliefs and practices to produce Candomble. Although far less known in North America than either Vodou or Santeria, Candomble never had to operate in secret in its native Brazil. An urban religion, it is divided into various houses, known as *terrenos*, each made up of familial and spiritual lineages. The newer Brazilian NRMs of Macumba and Umbanda began in the 1920s in Rio as deliberate attempts to demystify Candomble and to synthesize a Brazilian national religion. Today, these religions are practiced by millions of mostly poor Brazilians in cities across the country.

African NRMs in North America

In the Protestant-dominant areas of the United States and the British Caribbean, Africans were often unable to retain their own language, live freely in cities, or gather socially with their fellow Africans. As a result, new religions from this part of the African Diaspora developed much more slowly than they did in Catholic Haiti, Cuba, and Brazil, and took different forms. Most Black people in these areas converted to Protestantism. Although there were independent Black denominations that maintained a trace of African worship practices, such as joyous singing and clapping, these were never considered heretical or in tension with society by the religious and political establishment, and thus cannot be considered as New Religious Movements.

When Black NRMs did arise in the United States and Jamaica in the early twentieth century, they did not emphasize a West African pantheon of spirits. Rather, they grew out of African nationalism. This nationalist spirit is no coincidence but testifies to the importance of Marcus Garvey (1887–1940), the Jamaican-born leader of the "Back to Africa" movement. In 1914 he founded the Universal Negro Improvement Association, which claimed six million members at its peak. Garvey stressed Black pride and self-esteem, and advocated that Africans from all over the world should unite in their common heritage and separate from White society.

Garvey's message was not specifically religious, but it did bear a messianic tone. He portrayed the return to Africa as salvation from racism and injustice, a kind of ascension to a purer realm. Garvey thus influenced many subsequent New Religious Movements, which saw Africa as a sacred land, and he attracted followers—known as "Garveyites"—who preached his message with religious fervor.

Rastafarianism

The religious appropriation of Garvey's teachings can be seen in a prophecy that was attributed to him: in Africa a king would be crowned who would serve as a redeemer. This message rose to prominence when, in 1930, Ras Tafari Makonnen (1891–1975) ascended to the throne in Ethiopia. Taking the name Haile Selassie I, he claimed a biblical lineage along with the titles "King of Kings" and "Lion of Judah." Outside of Ethiopia, these religious associations spawned a small group of followers in Jamaica, and in the 1950s the movement began to grow rapidly in size. The **Rastafarian** message of the imminent return to Africa as the Promised Land resonated among the poorer classes in Jamaica, and later the movement spread into the middle classes and abroad, especially to Africa itself.

Rastafarianism has become widely known through the popularity of reggae music, where numerous adherents such as Bob Marley have played foundational roles. Famous for its use of marijuana as a spiritual sacrament and medicine, as well as for the distinctive dreadlocks worn by its followers, Rastafarianism holds to an ethics of natural living (often involving vegetarianism, growing organic foods, and other dietary prescriptions) and promotes an intuitive and personal reading of the Bible. Official Rastafarian holy days, including the anniversaries of Haile Selassie's birth and coronation, are celebrated by dancing and chanting parties known as bingis.

CLOSE-UP

The Kimbanguist Church

The Kimbanguist Church, founded in 1921 in the Congo, is the largest African Initiated Church, with some ten million members. Its founder, Simon Kimbangu (1887–1951), was educated at a Baptist mission near his home of N'Kamba. Receiving his call in April 1921, he began his healing ministry not as a traditional healer but through invoking the power of Christ. The Church arose in part in response to the 1918 worldwide influenza epidemic; the epidemic's high death toll in Africa seemed to deepen a growing distrust of missionaries. Vast numbers of Congolese came to N'Kamba to be cured, and a few months later the Belgian colonial authorities arrested Kimbangu on suspicion of fomenting rebellion. He was condemned to death but his sentence was later commuted to life imprisonment; he remained in prison until his death in 1951. While incarcerated, Kimbangu is said to have miraculously visited his followers, who were seen as subversive and were persecuted by the Belgian government throughout the 1950s.

Thanks to the leadership of Kimbangu's wife, Muilu Marie (1885–1959), the Church grew and organized despite Simon's imprisonment and death. In 1956 it formally incorporated as a religion, and in 1969 was admitted as a member of the World Council of Churches, cementing the Church's "middle-class" aspirations. Today the Kimbanguist Church runs schools and hospitals in the Congo, where its Sunday services include biblically based sermons, and hymns comprising Kimbangu's teachings set to music. Some controversy still clings to the Church, centered on whether Simon Kimbangu was in fact the messiah. Kimbangu's successors have also on occasion made ambiguous claims to divinity.

An African man wears a T-shirt with the image of the Congolese prophet Simon Kimbangu, the founder of the largest African Initiated Church.

Nation of Islam

The Nation of Islam, despite its name, derived less from traditional Islam than from Black Nationalism. Originating in Detroit around 1930 with a mysterious figure named W.D. Fard, this budding religious movement drew on the teachings of Garvey and others to offer a distinctive religious basis to conceptions of African racial superiority. The Nation of Islam thereby provided an alternative religiosity with respect to the Black denominations within the Christian tradition which, from the perspective of Nation of Islam adherents, had been irrevocably tainted with the sins of the White race. Around 1934, Fard designated Elijah Poole as his successor, renaming him Elijah Muhammad, and then disappeared. Muhammad then revealed that Fard was in fact God and that he, Elijah Muhammad, had been selected as his Prophet. Appropriating and reversing nineteenth-century (White, Anglo-European) race theory, Elijah Muhammad and the Nation of Islam developed a theology of Black superiority and demonized the White race as inferior and inherently malicious. As the Nation of Islam grew in prominence through the mid-twentieth century, taking on Malcolm X as one of its most famous adherents, it came into more regular contact with traditional Islam. In the late twentieth century the Nation split into factions, with many of its adherents eventually being absorbed into traditional Islam (the teachings of which are devoid of race theory) while others retained a separate and distinct religious identity.

Rastafarianism and Nation of Islam are two groups that find common inspiration in Black Nationalism combined with the claim to an original and true form of Black spirituality. Like other NRMs of the African diaspora, they thus show creativity in developing powerful religious responses to the cultural situation of racism and the legacy of slavery.

Islam is not often seen as a source of New Religious Movements. Whether represented positively (as "the religion of peace") or negatively (as "a religion of fanatics"), Islam is usually characterized in Western media as a monolithic, unchanging religion. This is an oversimplification based not only on the West's general

 ignorance of Islam but also on Islam's own self-representation to outsiders. A number of New Religious Movements have in fact arisen from Islam. This chapter will, after a brief theoretical and historical treatment, focus on the two tendencies within Islam that have given rise to many of these NRMs: the mystical and the fundamentalist.

Islam is the second largest religion in the world after Christianity. Muslims are generally divided into **Sunnis**, who make up 85–90% of all Muslims, and **Shiites**, who live in almost all countries with a Muslim population but form the majority in only four: Iran, Bahrain, Iraq, and Azerbaijan. All Muslims worship God (in Arabic, *Allah*) according to the Holy Book he gave to all humanity, the Quran, which was revealed to the prophet Muhammad (c. 570–c. 632). Muslims date the founding of their religion to the year 622, when Muhammad established a community of believers in Medina.

Like Christianity, Islam is a universalist religion that places emphasis on correct belief, and thus also like Christianity, it has produced many sects and heresies. Works detailing (and condemning) various Islamic "heresies" have been written from the ninth century until today. In fact, as scholars learn more about the early history of Islam, it becomes apparent that these "heretical sects" were instrumental in the peaceful spread of Islam to non-Arab peoples. Mark Sedgwick, a professor of Islamic history and contemporary religious movements, has analyzed Arabic words that classify religion in order to find their closest parallel with Western sociological terms.[1] Based on his research, he asserts that one can indeed look at Islam through the lens of NRM studies. Specifically, Sedgwick notes that in classical sociology of religion, the word "denomination" is used for a religious institution in low tension with society. In Arabic, this concept is best equated with the term *madhhab*, a school of legal interpretation. There are four main *madhhabs* in Sunni Islam, which differ not only in terms of how strictly or liberally they interpret the law but also by region. Muslims generally follow whichever *madhhab* they were raised in, so a Malaysian Muslim would likely be a Shafiite, whereas a Muslim born in southern Egypt would likely be a Malikite. *Madhhabs* mutually recognize each other as legitimate, much as mainstream Protestant denominations do.

By way of contrast, Sedgwick defines the Arabic word *firqa* as "an organized sectarian body that claims a monopoly over the proper interpretation of Islam." Thus, like the Western concept of sect, a *firqa* actively seeks converts and is in high tension with its environment. *Firqas* have been recognized as a problem within Islam from the beginning. Indeed, Muhammad is said to have predicted them. The exclusive truth claims of *firqas* often derive from one of two sources: the desire to return to a "pure," "original" Islam, or the belief in an authentic inspired leader. The Kharijites, who broke with Islam shortly after Muhammad's death, are generally considered to be the first *firqa*. Known as "leavers" or "dissenters," they were worried that the expansion of Islam would sully its initial purity. One sect within the Kharijites, the Ibadis, has survived to this day.

The next great *firqa*, at least by Sunni standards, is Shiite Islam. Shiites, of course, see themselves as true Islam and the Sunnis as misguided. The Sunni–Shiite split can be traced to a crisis of succession in early Islam. Muhammad left strict orders that his son-in-law, Ali, was to serve as his successor. After Ali was killed by a Khajirite, some Muslims accepted non-hereditary political rulers, known as caliphs, as legitimate. They sought spiritual guidance from the oral tradition of Muhammad's words and actions, known as the Sunna. Other Muslims, who called themselves the Shia Islam, the Party of Ali, believed that only Ali's descendants were chosen by God to be Muhammad's legitimate heirs, called imams. The martyrdom of Ali's son-in-law Husayn, the Third Imam, by the ruling caliphs at the Battle of Karbala in 680, has become a central event in the construction of Shiite identity. According to Shiite theology, the Twelfth Imam never died but has been "occluded" or hidden from human history, and will one day reappear in the form of the Mahdi (the guided one), a messiah figure who will enact a reign of justice.

Throughout Islamic history, several *firqas* have arisen that derive their authority from a leader who claims to be the Mahdi, and is worshipped as divine. As Islam is supremely suspicious of idolatry, these movements were quickly condemned as heresy and suppressed. Some of the more recent Mahdi-inspired groups include followers of a Shiite Muslim, Mirza Ali Muhammad (1819–1850), who declared himself the missing Twelfth Imam, and called himself the Bab-ud-Din, or "the Gate of Faith," a reference to the fact that the Shiite imams were called "gates" because believers passed through them to gain access to true faith. These followers, known as Babis, organized themselves in Iran in 1844. A combination of religious and political forces in Iran executed the Bab and suppressed the Babi movement. But the story does not end here: one Babi went on to found the Baha'i faith, which will be discussed in the Close-up feature (p. 102).

Sunni theology also includes the idea of Mahdi, though not as the Twelfth Imam returned. In 1881 in the Sudan, a religious and political leader named Muhammad ibn Abdalla (1844–1885) proclaimed himself the Mahdi and started a *firqa* known as the Ansars, who took over the capital, Khartoum, in 1885. Today the Ansars are an important force in Sudanese politics and number approximately three million.

The Ahmadiyya movement began in 1899, when a South Asian Muslim named Mirza Ghulam Ahmad (1835–1908) announced he was the Mahdi. Because of this claim, the Ahmadiyyas were declared to be non-Muslim and brutally persecuted in Muslim India (modern Pakistan) even as they maintained the beliefs and practices of Sunni Islam. Today the Ahmadiyya movement has around ten million followers and supports educational and social reform in Islamic countries as well as interfaith movements in the West.

Other *firqas* eschew divinely inspired leaders and call for a new Islam based on "strict" interpretation of the Quran. Of these the most famous is Al-Qaeda which, along with its precursors such as Wahhabism and the Muslim Brotherhood, will be discussed later.

Mystical Islamic NRMs: Sufism

In the ninth century, caliphs in Baghdad ruled the Islamic world. As Islam expanded its territory and developed a political structure, Baghdad became a city of material grandeur and ritual pomp. These are the circumstances that gave birth to the Sufi movement (in Arabic, *tasawwuf*). Like other Islamic movements, Sufism looked to the origins of Islam. What they saw there was an emphasis on austere inward-looking contemplation, and thus the Sufis rejected the growing legalistic and the worldly tendencies in Islam.

Sufism became a broad and diverse movement, but at the heart of it is the quest for mystical unity, the experience of being "one with God." This feeling led Sufis to the realization that everything is part of God, including themselves. This idea presented a theological problem to the orthodox Islamic caliphs, who in the early tenth century began executing Sufi leaders. Thus, Sufi organizations went underground.

In the twelfth century Sufis began to organize themselves into spiritual fraternities, centered on a living saint (*pir* or *shaikh*). Sufi orders are called *tariqas* (path) and have something of the connotation of Catholic monastic orders, but Sufis neither take vows of celibacy nor do they necessarily remove themselves from society. Indeed some Sufi orders encourage their members to live outwardly unremarkable lives while inwardly pursuing a spiritual path. A Sufi initiate, known as a fakir or dervish, may engage in a variety of ascetic practices, including meditation, singing, and dancing, in order to achieve an ecstatic trance. An independent spiritual leader heads each order, and each has a different set of practices.

Like the Kharijites and early Shiites, Sufis were effective missionaries and had particular success in spreading Islam in sub-Saharan Africa and Central and Southeast Asia. Today Sufi orders are found in every part of the Muslim world, often developing local traditions centered on the shrine of the founder of the order.

In the last hundred years, Sufi masters have begun reaching out to the West as Sufism has become a new "counter-cultural religion." The man who paved the way for the Western presence of Sufism was Hazrat Inayat Khan (1882–1927). A Muslim scholar and musician influenced by Hindu mystics, Khan left his native India to settle in the West in 1910 and there founded the Sufi Order, which emphasized the validity of all world religions and taught various healing practices. Now known as the Sufi Order International, the movement was revitalized in the 1960s by Khan's son, Pir Vilayat Khan (1916–2004). Many members of Kahn's Sufi Order would consider themselves Sufis but not Muslims, an identification that would be contradictory to Muslim members of Sufi orders.

Since then virtually every major Sufi order has established some degree of presence in the West. For example, Shaikh Nazim (1922–), the current leader of the Haqqani Naqshbandis, a very devout Sufi order, began visiting London in 1973 and the U.S. in 1991, where the order now has a public presence in the form of the Haqqani Foundation. While a faithful Muslim, Shaikh Nazim has taught many Westerners his order's ecstatic practices without requiring their conversion to Islam first.

Thanks to Sufi masters such as these, a more universal Sufism entered the global New Age and took its place among Western esoteric groups and NRMs from Asia. In fact, there are some striking parallels between Sufi movements in the West and the NRMs discussed in Chapters 3 and 4. Sufi wisdom often teaches a hidden knowledge, available only to insiders, similar to Gnosticism. Like Hindu gurus and Buddhist masters in the West, Sufi shaikhs (spiritual masters) are often charismatic, appealingly "exotic" and "authentic" non-Westerners, who emphasize the personal transmission of religious knowledge between master and student.

Some new religions in the West have quite tenuous connections with Sufism, but seem to be inspired by, or have borrowed from, the tradition. For example, Meher Baba (1894–1969) is a South Asian guru who was considered an avatar (manifestation) of God and spent most of his life under a vow of silence. His own God-realization was precipitated by his encounter with a female Sufi master in 1913. After Baba visited the United States as one of Hazrat Khan's first American disciples, he formed the group known as Sufism Reorganized. Today Meher Baba still has a small number of devotees in the West, who see him as the religious master of the ages.

Revivalism and Scriptural Fundamentalism

The term **fundamentalism** was originally coined to describe a conservative backlash in American Protestantism. This movement took its name from twelve pamphlets called "The Fundamentals," which were distributed to churches between 1910 and 1915. The most important fundamentalist beliefs include the inerrancy of Scripture, the continuity between religion and politics, and the evil nature of the secular state. Recently, the word fundamentalism has been attached to Hindu, Sikh, Buddhist, and Jewish groups with various degrees of applicability. And of course, the word has become practically synonymous with certain strains of Islam, first appearing as "Islamic fundamentalism" in connection with the 1979 Iranian Revolution, when a secular Western-supported monarchy was overthrown by conservative Shiite Muslim clerics.

Islamic "fundamentalists" have much in common with their Christian counterparts, including a desire to return to religious origins through a literal interpretation of Scripture, and anger at modernity and secularism (in Islam, often manifested as a rage at the West). However, in general the term "Islamic fundamentalism" conceals more than it reveals. Behind that phrase is a series of Islamic movements, some with little in common but all at one time in tension with their surrounding society and the established religion. In other words, they can be usefully analyzed as New Religious Movements.

The Wahhabi movement began in the 1740s in the Arabian Peninsula, when Muhammad ibn Abd-al-Wahhab (1703–1791) became outraged by the prevalence of Sufi shrines and pilgrimage routes on the peninsula, which he saw as un-Islamic folk religion or even idolatry. Wahhab's influence grew through his sermons preached to pilgrims at Mecca. Based on the Hanbalite *madhhab*, the most literalistic of the four schools of interpretation, Wahhabi Islam advocated a return to the pure Islam of Muhammad's day. As a school of legal interpretation Wahhabism is extremely critical of any perceived innovation within Islam. Because Wahhabism is exclusive, universalist, and often in tension with greater Islamic society, it is best considered a *firqa*, not a *madhhab*.

Wahhabism became identified with the Saud family of the Arabian Peninsula. When, in 1932, the family became rulers of a newly unified Saudi Arabia, Wahhabism was enshrined as the dominant ideology. When the Saudis began exporting oil in the mid-twentieth century, their newly emerging financial power allowed the Wahhabi movement to fund mosques and schools all over the world; in 1979 the Saudi royal family officially turned over all education in Saudi Arabia to the Wahhabi movement, thereby all but assuring its continuing influence on Saudi youth. Wahhabism's influence around the Muslim world has increased still further in recent years; it can be seen in situations as diverse as the campaign against Sufi orders in the former Soviet republics of Central Asia and the proliferation of anti-Western literature in American mosques. Despite (or, perhaps, because of) Wahhabism's global reach and financial clout, other

Muslims see this movement as a fringe group, an inauthentic and dangerous form of Islam. Muslims excoriate Wahhabis for their past enslavement of Turkish Muslims, and for inspiring present-day acts of indiscriminate murder.

Wahhabism also helped influence the growth of a series of *firqas* sometimes known collectively as the **Islamist** movement. Since the time of the Crusades (eleventh–fourteenth centuries) there has existed a train of Muslim Arab thought that has seen the West as imperialist and immoral. But in the twentieth century, the fall of the Ottoman Empire, the emigration of European Jews to Palestine, and the breakdown of traditional Middle Eastern society energized this way of thinking and produced the first Islamist groups. The Muslim Brotherhood was founded in 1928 in Egypt by Hassan al-Banna (1906–1949) and advocated a "restoration" of the Quran, while appealing to urban, educated classes. The Brotherhood worked towards a "re-Islamization" of their community and then all of Egypt through a program of educational, charitable, and welfare activity. Members actively fought against both "superstitions" (such as popular folk magic) and the modernization of daily life.

By 1954 more than a half million Egyptians were active members of the Brotherhood, a number that alarmed Egypt's newly installed government, which was socialist and secular. The Brotherhood was persecuted, but this only made it split into new factions. One of these, the Islamic Jihad, began a campaign of assassinating Egyptian political figures, culminating in the murder of President Anwar Sadat in 1981.

The Islamic Jihad justified their campaign of violence by invoking the works of the primary theorist of Islamism: Abdul Ala Mawdudi (1903–1979), a prolific writer from South Asia and founder of his own Islamist movement, Jamaat-e-Islami. It was he who first articulated the doctrine of jihad, a term from the Quran literally meaning "inner struggle," as a political duty. Mawdudi theorized that it was every Muslim's individual obligation to wrest authority from the forces opposing Islam, including Muslim leaders deemed insufficiently pure. Mawdudi thought new governments should be re-established modeled on early Muslim states.

By the 1980s, Islamist movements had a fully formed ideology that justified terrorism. This ideology beseeched all devout Muslims to wage war on anyone who threatened Islam, including Muslim governments that were not following Muslim law. It explicitly allowed for the murder of civilians, including women and children, despite strict injunctions against just that in the Quran and the Sunna.

Al-Qaeda as NRM

The most notorious group to enact this new concept of jihad is Al-Qaeda, which was founded in 1989 by Osama bin Laden (1957–). The son of a wealthy businessman in Saudi Arabia, bin Laden received a typical Wahhabi education. He learned his political and strategic skills when in 1980 he moved to Afghanistan to fight the Soviet invasion. There he began an international network to support the struggle. With the withdrawal of the Soviets in 1989 and the placement of American troops in Saudi Arabia due to Iraq's invasion of Kuwait, bin Laden's mission became increasingly anti-American, and anti-Saudi government. Bin Laden moved back to Afghanistan in 1996 to support its new Islamist government, the Taliban, by supplying weapons and building mosques, while also planning terrorist attacks on the West and forming alliances with Islamist groups all over the world.

Since the September 11, 2001 terrorist attacks on the United States, Al-Qaeda has been extensively studied in the West. One issue that has been discussed often is the nature of the relationship between Al-Qaeda and Islam in general. Neither of the two typical strategies used to explain this relationship are satisfactory. One argument, heard immediately after the terrorist outrages and still voiced among extreme right-wing commentators, is that Al-Qaeda is representative of Islam in general, which is portrayed as a violent religion dedicated to jihad or "Holy War" against all non-Muslims. The other rhetorical strategy is that Al-Qaeda is motivated by an irrational hatred of freedom (and/or the West and/or America) and that its doctrines and practices have no connection whatsoever with mainstream Islam, which is a religion of peace.

Both approaches are overly simplistic. Scholars continue to debate the most productive way to analyze Al-Qaeda. Some have argued it should be studied as a product of a post-modern Media Age. Others maintain that it functions as an NRM whose parent religion is Islam. Islamist movements like Al-Qaeda exist in tension with the political authorities of the countries in which they were founded as well as with the West. Mark Sedgwick argues that these movements should be counted as *firqas*. In particular, Al-Qaeda "displays almost all the characteristics of the *firqa*. It is outward-oriented. Membership

CLOSE-UP

Baha'i

Baha'i is an NRM that began as a *firqa* within Shiite Islam and now has some claim to the title of world religion. Baha'i begins after the suppression of the messianic sect of Shiite Islam known as Babism (see p. 96), when one of the Bab's disciples had a revelation in 1853 that he was the promised one foretold by the Bab. Calling himself Baha'u'llah (1817–1892), or "Glory of God," the prophet and his followers—called Baha'is—were persecuted in Persia, exiled to Iraq, and then placed under house arrest in various cities throughout the Ottoman Empire. Baha'u'llah spent the last twenty-four years of his life in the Ottoman prison city of Acre (today near Haifa, in Israel).

Leadership of Baha'i passed to Baha'u'llah's son, then to his great-grandson. Since 1963, Baha'is have been governed by the Universal House of Justice, a nine-man elected international body, considered to be guided by God and infallible, which resides in Haifa close to Baha'i holy sites.

Propagated by volunteer missionaries, the Baha'i faith has become one of the most widespread religions on earth, active in over two hundred countries. Baha'i must operate underground in many Muslim countries, especially in its birthplace of Iran, where it has been brutally repressed. Baha'i first came to the United States in 1894, and today the faith has 150,000 American adherents, out of a total membership of approximately five million. From the 1960s onwards, the social base of the religion shifted to the developing world, especially India, Malaysia, the Pacific Islands, Latin America, and Africa.

The central belief of the Baha'i faith is the unity of all religions. Baha'u'llah is said to be the latest, but not the last, in the long line of prophets of God, including Muhammad of course, but also Moses, Jesus, and the Buddha. Each prophet is superseded by the next. This belief has made the Baha'is natural proponents of globalism, as shown in their motto, "The earth is but one country, and mankind its citizens," and put into practice by their campaigns for racial and social justice. Baha'is have built one worship center on each continent; each one has nine sides, and is open for all to worship. Ultimately, it seeks a world government and a world language.

Baha'is have their own calendar, consisting of nineteen months each with nineteen days. Congregations (called Local Spiritual Assemblies) hold services, which are closed to non-Baha'is and usually take place at members' homes on the first day of each Baha'i month.

In many ways, Baha'i is a typical NRM, showing tensions with its parent religion and with the social environment that produced it. But just how close Baha'i is to Islam remains a controversial issue. In general, the Baha'i faith follows an interpretation of Islamic (in particular Shiite) theology and prophecy, most notably sharing with Islam the idea that history will reveal the will of God in the form of a comprehensive legal system to regulate society.

Baha'is' ritual life is rooted in Islam. One month of the Baha'i calendar is set aside for fasting from sunup until sundown, similar to the Muslim month of Ramadan. Like Islam, the Baha'i faith has five obligatory prayers daily (although Baha'is may choose among them). Baha'is are also encouraged to make a pilgrimage to the Baha'i world center in Haifa (mirroring the Muslim pilgrimage to Mecca), and donate a percentage of their income to charity.

Despite this apparent commonality, the Baha'i faith stresses its claim as a new revelation independent from Islam, noting that Muslims do not recognize Baha'i as a sect of Islam (but neither do they recognize Ahmadiyya, nor in some cases Wahhabism). In point of fact, many Baha'i converts have little idea of its Islamic background. In the United States, early missionaries portrayed Baha'i as the fulfillment of Christianity. Indeed the first Baha'i teacher in the U.S. used the Bible to "prove" that Baha'u'llah was the return of Jesus. Today, most recent Baha'i converts are former Christians, Hindus, or practitioners of indigenous religion. Since most of the early Baha'i missionaries were North Americans, the Baha'i faith, as it spread, tended to be initially perceived as a "Western" rather than an Islamic religion.

View of the upper terraced gardens and the shrine of the Bab, part of the religious and administrative center of the Baha'i religion situated on Mount Carmel in Haifa, Israel.

Whether it can be considered an Islamic *firqa* or not, Baha'i, by combining Islam's elements of universalism and ritual life with the nineteenth century's liberal theology and evolutionary theory of religion, has become a NRM success story, a truly global religion. Like all religions, Baha'i has spawned its own breakaway sects—small groups of Baha'is who call themselves "Orthodox" and do not recognize the Universal House of Justice.

is voluntary and a primary source of its members' identity. It is exclusive and organized, and the possibility of discipline clearly exists."[2]

Like some other NRMs, Al-Qaeda has Utopian or even apocalyptic ideology. While older Islamist groups targeted local governments, Al-Qaeda instead aimed for nothing less than the complete revolutionary transformation of the world, and thus attacked what they saw as the touchstones of all evil: the United States, its international presence, and the system of world capitalism. Indeed, Al-Qaeda's master plan is said to predict the re-establishment of the Caliphate, an international Islamic state, by the year 2016. After that it is claimed there will be a period of "total confrontation" between "the believers and the non-believers."[3] Fortunately, Al-Qaeda's rhetoric, like that of many NRMs, bears little resemblance to reality.

Also like many other NRMs, Al-Qaeda is led by a charismatic master. Osama bin Laden is neither a trained theologian nor a political theorist (although other Al-Qaeda leaders are). The widely distributed images of Osama wearing a turban and simple robe and living in a cave, as Muhammad did as he received the Quran, would carry an iconographic resonance for many Muslims.

In 1967, a philosophy professor in his mid-thirties resigned from his teaching post at the University of Jabalpur in India and opened an ashram where he taught a religious practice known as "dynamic meditation," which included spontaneous shouting and dancing. Adding two honorific titles to his given name of "Rajneesh," the Bhagwan  Shree Rajneesh held views that offended many Indians while appealing to Western hippies and spiritual experimenters visiting India. In 1981 he moved to the U.S. and set up a commune known as Rajneeshpuram near the town of Antelope, Oregon. Known as the "sex guru" for his message that sex was a path to liberation, Rajneesh became notorious for his conflicts with the surrounding town and his daily rides in his many Rolls-Royces. In 1987 Rajneesh's visa was revoked and he returned to his ashram in India. The following year he changed his name to the more neutral sounding Osho. He died in 1990, but the Osho Commune lives on in India to this day.

At first glance, it may seem that Osho fits into the "New Religion as Asian Mission to the West" model that was the theme of Chapter 4. In fact Osho is an example of a more recent, and more prevalent, phenomenon. Although Osho was known as a popularizer of **Tantric** Hinduism, his teachings originated not from India or anyplace else but from his eclectic interests, which included world philosophy, Zen Buddhism, and a range of self-improvement techniques.

Upon his return to India Rajneesh remade himself, casting aside his image as "sex guru" and the authoritarian structure of Rajneeshpuram, instead advocating a global religion of kindness and self-transformation. The Osho organization currently runs meditation centers in several dozen countries, from Argentina to Zimbabwe, coordinated through the office of Osho Global Connections. The organization's primary center, Osho Multiversity in Pune, India, calls itself "the largest center in the world for meditation and personal growth processes." The historian of religion Hugh Urban writes that it "teaches a dizzying array of spiritual techniques drawn from a smorgasbord of traditions: astrology training, Feldenkrais bodywork, crystal energy, acupuncture, neo-Zen and other New Age activities [...] and markets it to a global audience of spiritual consumers."[1] Osho is a religion that is only possible in the twenty-first century: a truly global NRM.

The story of Osho demonstrates that to understand the direction NRMs are moving in today and to venture any sort of prediction about where NRMs will be tomorrow, we must take into account the process of globalization. It seems that everyone is talking about this powerful force in today's world, even if nobody can agree on a definition. At the very least, globalization means the interconnection of worldwide social, economic, and cultural structures. This chapter first argues that NRMs are essentially global in nature and then goes on to examine two instances in which that nature is revealed: NRMs' use of the Internet, and NRMs and violence. The conclusion to this chapter will examine what the global nature of NRMs can tell us about their future.

NRMs and Globalization

The word "globalization" often conjures up images of multinational corporations, globally recognized consumer products such as McDonald's hamburgers or Nike sneakers, and worldwide financial institutions like the International Monetary Fund (IMF) or the World Bank. Religions, in our popular imagination, are seen as the most traditional part of our culture (maybe that's why they're called religious "traditions") and the least likely institutions to be agents of globalization. Religions must stand in opposition to whatever it is the Big Mac or the IMF stand for.

Nothing could be further from the truth. Religions were among the first agents of globalization and have contributed to the exchange and interconnection of ideas, people, and objects for thousands of years. As we saw in previous chapters, as early as the first century C.E., Buddhist missionaries traveled along the Silk Road, one of the first "global information highways." Beginning in the fifteenth century, Christianity spread throughout the Americas and Africa by adapting (and being adapted by) local traditions. Religions have always been in the process of interacting, expanding, synthesizing, borrowing, and changing. In short, they are deeply involved in the process of globalization. NRMs are at the vanguard of this process, and it might be argued that NRMs by their very nature are agents of globalization.

The Canadian scholars Irving Hexham and Carla Poewe have advanced an interesting thesis: that NRMs take elements of folk religions—local customs that are not part of any "world religion"—and standardize and internationalize them to produce what they call a "global folk culture." According to Hexham and Poewe, what someone like Rajneesh produces and distributes globally is "a fragment of a tradition intent, first, on fragmenting other traditions and then on uniting with these fragments to bear new fruit in the soil of a distinct folk religion." These new fruit are "new religions, authenticated by specific local folk religions [which] are a response to urban sophisticates' deep yearnings for global folk religions."[2]

Hexham and Poewe give us the example of Emanuel Swedenborg who, as we saw in Chapter 3, was one of the key figures in the popularization and eventual globalization of Western esotericism. It is possible that he borrowed some of his visualization techniques and theories about multiple worlds from the shamanic practices of the indigenous people of Sweden. Today, Western esotericism forms the nucleus of the international New Age culture, which can be found from Brazil to Japan. Other examples of local traditions that have become globalized include Mormonism, drawn in part from Euro-American folk magic, and Soka Gakkai, based on the most nativistic of all Japanese Buddhist sects. Both now have a presence in hundreds of countries.

Another example would be Chinese NRMs. No longer merely a factor in China, they are truly globalized, via the flow of Chinese immigrants and ideas. The body-cultivation techniques of qigong masters are no longer the exclusive knowledge of a certain Daoist lineage to be practiced by a few people on one mountain in China.

NRMs represent a further shift in the nature of religious communities from the local to the global. Organizations like Osho, Soka Gakkai, the Unification Church, Baha'i, and the various groups that make up the New Age are of course international, with a presence in many countries. But more than that, their ethic is global: they are among the first organizations of any kind to advocate the ideals of world citizenship, of the end of nationalism, and of seeking spiritual solutions to global problems. All the organizations mentioned above, in different ways, cultivate members who see themselves as "citizens of the world" and look forward to the birth of a global

"New Age" (in which they are destined to play a crucial role), when global fragmentation can end and the healing of the world can begin.

In fact this ethic of globalization can function as a response to the very same social tension that defines NRMs. When Osho, Soka Gakkai, and many other NRMs are accused of being unacceptably different, heretical, or dangerous, they may, as British sociologist James A. Beckford puts it, "justify their claim to freedom by arguing that human history has been unfolding in a providential fashion and that the moment has come to sweep away outdated religious beliefs and practices in order to usher in a new universal dispensation."[3]

Of course, for many NRMs, this "new universal dispensation" (a dispensation is a divine ordering of worldly affairs) is not a harmonious ethic of globalization. As we have seen, some NRMs are explicitly anti-global. Al-Qaeda, most notably, has waged religious war against the very symbols of globalization (as it sees it) including American embassies abroad, the headquarters of the U.S. military complex, and of course, the center of "World Trade." Other NRMs refute globalization non-violently by invoking nativist or nationalist concerns. Rastafarianism, for example, sanctifies "native" (i.e. non-White) Jamaican culture while seeking redemption through African nationalism.

But NRMs that reject globalization use globalized methods. Al-Qaeda's 9/11 attacks used the fruits of globalization (open national borders, inexpensive air travel, Internet and cell phone communication) to attack it. Today, Al-Qaeda remains a threat to the West in part because it operates as semi-independent cells all over the world, a truly globalized presence. And as we saw in Chapter 6, Rastafarianism, thanks in part to the commercial production and distribution of reggae music, has also become an NRM with global scope.

NRMs, whether they invoke or decry a global ethic, are part of a larger reconfiguring of the place of religions in the world. As religion is being displaced from its traditional location in communal and social identity, it becomes more privatized and individualist, located in the realm of individual choice. This does not mean religious communities are no longer important or prevalent, of course, but that they have become voluntary and non-localized. NRMs are not the only example of these new kinds of religious communities, but they are the most visible, and they have been by necessity the most international. Practitioners of Santeria, paganism, or Sufism might feel they have more in common with the fellow practitioners who live on the other side of the world than they do with their next-door neighbors. Joining an NRM often means increased opportunity for travel and interaction with people from other parts of the world. Members of NRMs can choose to live scattered across decentralized international communities, as does the Family (the Children of God), or they can choose to relocate *en masse* for any number of reasons, as when 150 members of the Taiwanese UFO group Chen Tao moved to California in 1995 and then to Texas in 1997 to fulfill the group leader's prophecy.

Global connections: NRMs and the Internet

The Internet, of course, has brought about a communications revolution. The way new religions have explored the possibilities of the World Wide Web makes other institutions seem antiquated by comparison. NRMs used Internet communication, such as electronic bulletin boards and online chat rooms, even before the popularization of the Web in the late 1990s. Internet communication establishes a feeling of community among dispersed or isolated members. Websites provide an official presence in cyberspace and an easy way to disseminate information. But websites cannot be relied upon as indicative of the popularity of NRMs. For example, Scientology, a religion with only a few tens of thousands of members worldwide, has a website as extensive, and as professional looking, as that of the Catholic Church, which has a billion adherents. There seem to be as many websites for Pagans as there are for Protestants. Indeed, one recent study has found over ten thousand Pagan sites on the Internet, representing everything from **covens** that perform virtual rituals to solitary witches seeking companionship online.[4]

The special relationship between NRMs and the Web was first widely noticed in March 1997 after the Heaven's Gate suicide (see p. 46), when it was revealed that some members had outside jobs designing websites. The group's own website became the focus of media attention as a "recruitment site" for new members. Predictably, the anticult movement expressed alarm that the World Wide Web (still a new phenomenon in 1997) would be used for NRM recruitment, and the media picked up on this story. The fear that the Web could seduce naive web-users into joining suicide cults was exacerbated by the fact that the stereotype of the typical heavy Web user matched that of the typical NRM member: young, well educated, with few responsibilities or social attachments.

Scholars have rejected this "Internet as recruitment tool" argument convincingly. They have demonstrated that joining a new religion is a social process, involving networks of friends or family. NRM websites may be interactive in theory, and might be filled with attractive images and text, but it is hard to imagine anyone joining an NRM after simply surfing its website any more than they would after reading a pamphlet or watching a video.

Certainly the Internet is the best way for NRMs to disseminate information. Students writing an essay or journalists researching an article about an NRM naturally turn to the Internet first. NRMs also use the Internet to their advantage by keeping in touch with scholars, public advocates, or other groups interested in protecting freedom of religion. But reliance on the Internet has its disadvantages as well. As James A. Beckford writes, "NRMs that rely heavily on the Web as a means of informing the public about their beliefs and practices run the risk that opponents, apostates, and ruthless competitors will steal or parody their material."[5] He also notes that anticult and countercult movements have active web presences as well, and using search engines to seek out NRM homepages will often direct the searcher to anticult websites.

More important than listing the advantages and disadvantages of the Internet is understanding how the Internet is changing the very nature of NRMs. The Internet has been a site for the constant reinvention of spiritual practice. Through linked websites, chat rooms, and live webcams, new ritual communities can form that are entirely virtual. These can include online-only NRMs such as Western Reform Taoism, "joke" or parody religions such as the Church of Moo, or religions that exist in physical space but also have virtual temples and conduct online ritual such as some pagan groups.

In theory at least, the rise of virtual ritual communities encourages the democratization of new religions. Boundaries of sex, race, age, or geography are now dissolvable, and the flow of information is more reversible (accessing and even creating websites is relatively inexpensive), allowing for the possibility of practices and doctrines being questioned anonymously. Ultimately, though, this Internet democracy may be harmful to the growth of NRMs. By disseminating techniques (from Zen meditation to Tantric sex) and information (from Gnostic revelations to Santeria pantheons), the Internet allows seekers to practice a variety of religions with the click of a mouse. Joining or committing becomes an option, and a quaint one at that.

Global Fears: NRMs and violence

If the 1990s witnessed the globalization of NRMs, they also saw a string of NRM-related violent incidents. As we saw in Chapter 2, a propensity for violence has been one of the accusations leveled against new religions for centuries. In the sixteenth century, the peace-loving Anabaptists were feared as violent fanatics. In the nineteenth-century United States, Catholics, Mormons, and Freemasons were often accused of committing murder and of being naturally bloodthirsty.

In our globalized world these accusations are rendered even more potent. NRM violence could happen at any time, anywhere, from suburban San Diego through a village in Africa to the Tokyo subway. Media turns a local incident into a global news story; experts who predict the next "killer cult" amplify fears.

Scholars who take a longer view have noted that NRMs must have four characteristics for them to be prone to violence: first, an apocalyptic belief in the imminent end of the world; second, a charismatic or even messianic leader; third, social and/or physical isolation; and fourth, most importantly, a sense of a looming showdown with the outside world, whether real or perceived.[6]

But these characteristics, especially the first three, are common to many NRMs (and, it might be argued, some evangelical Christian churches) that will never commit violent acts. Unfortunately, these four characteristics can identify a propensity for violence only after the fact; they have little predictive value. In any case, statistics demonstrate that NRMs are not inherently violent. Out of the tens of thousands of NRMs around the world, only six, as of 2005, have

Violence in New Religious Movements 1978–2005

NRM	DATE	LOCATION	NUMBER OF DEATHS
Peoples Temple	1978	Jonestown, Guyana	918 (mostly suicide)
Branch Davidians	1993	Waco, Texas	80 (murder-suicide)
Order of the Solar Temple	1994–97	Quebec, France, and Switzerland	74 (murder-suicide)
Aum Shinrikyo	1988–95	Japan	35 (murder)*
Heaven's Gate	1997	California	39 (suicide)
Movement for the Restoration of the Ten Commandments	2000	Uganda	780 (murder-suicide)

*Twelve subway-goers died from the sarin gas attack in 1995. Aum was responsible for at least twenty-three earlier murders, beginning in 1988.

engaged in homicidal or suicidal behavior (not counting Islamist movements). See the table on the previous page for details.

Why, then, does the "killer cult" stereotype persist? As discussed previously, "cult" is a constructed category, and violence is one of the main attributes of this construction. The anticult movement's argument is not that some NRMs are violent, but that any religion that engages in violence is by definition a "cult." The most famous case of NRM violence, and the reference point for all subsequent violent incidents, is the Peoples Temple mass murder/suicide in Jonestown, Guyana in 1978, where over nine hundred people died after consuming soft drinks laced with poison. Until the massacre, the Temple was not in fact considered an NRM but a progressive congregation within the mainstream Disciples of Christ denomination. A series of escalating government actions combined with tragic misunderstandings played into leader Jim Jones's millennial fears, causing the death of hundreds. The Branch Davidians, an offshoot of the Seventh-day Adventist family (a nineteenth-century millennialist sect that by the twentieth century had become a fairly mainstream denomination), were vilified as a "doomsday cult" as a lead-up to the fire that engulfed their compound in Waco, Texas in 1993. Researchers have shown that the heavy-handed techniques used by the FBI and the Bureau of Alcohol, Tobacco, and Firearms exacerbated an already explosive situation.[7]

This does not mean that NRMs never initiate violence; indeed it is safe to predict that an NRM will commit a violent act sooner or later somewhere in the world, just as it is safe to assume that an airplane will crash someplace, someday. Unfortunately, just as with airplanes, it is impossible to guess where and when an NRM will resort to violence. On the whole, though, NRMs are no more prone to violence than other religious or social organizations.

Is There a Future for NRMs?

Will NRMs play an influential role in the twenty-first century? We know that some of the most (in)famous NRMs, which became practically synonymous with negative "cult" stereotypes—such as the Unification Church, Hare Krishna, and Scientology—are slowly losing members. Recall, too, that the overall percentage of adherents of New Religious Movements in any given country remains steady.

The big religious stories of the twenty-first century, many observers feel, will be the continuing rise of the fundamentalist or conservative wings of established religions, the spread of Pentecostal and Charismatic Christianity, and continuing debate about immigration and security issues engendered by the place of Islam in the West.

Where does that leave NRMs? Will they continue to proliferate or will they be repressed into insignificance or non-existence? It is difficult to make confident predictions about the future of NRMs, in part because they exist in so many different situations all over the world. Although this book has focused in its first half on the West, and in its second half on East Asia, Africa and the African Diaspora, and the Islamic world, NRMs also play significant roles in other parts of the globe. South America has more—and more diverse—NRMs than might be expected. Brazil, especially, has not only seen a growth in Charismatic and Pentecostal churches but has a vibrant and diverse homegrown alternative spirituality, the growth of which has been referred to as the "Esoteric Boom." In Australia and New Zealand, meanwhile, NRMs are also on the rise—which could be either a cause or a symptom of falling rates of establishment church attendance. A general policy of multiculturalism in these countries also contributes to the spread of esoteric groups related to the New Age or to Neopaganism.

Elsewhere, NRMs are encountering greater legal and political opposition. New religions have been growing in the former Soviet Union and parts of Eastern Europe since the end of Communism in the early 1990s, despite opposition from the Orthodox Church and from the state. France is another country with an official policy that is explicitly hostile to new religions, in part because of its tradition of state-sponsored secularism. The French government has a taskforce—the Interministerial Mission on Watching and Combatting Sectarian Disorders—to keep an eye on NRMs, and in May 2001 passed a law that prohibited the location of NRMs near "sensitive places" such as schools and hospitals.[8] It may seem surprising that a liberal democracy like France has laws against "les sectes" (as they are called there) that are closer to those of China (discussed in Chapter 5) and Russia than those of the U.K. or the U.S. In France and Russia (and other parts of Europe to a certain extent), the argument is frequently made that NRMs are agents of American capitalism and imperialism, the spiritual equivalent of McDonalds: easily consumed, personally unhealthy, and destructive to indigenous culture. Some NRMs thus classified are indeed American-born (Scientology and Charismatic Christian churches, for example), but even those that are not (such as the Unification Church and Transcendental Meditation) have adopted American-style marketing techniques. NRMs can be used as further evidence in the argument that "globalization" is just a codeword for "Americanization."

Moreover, in many parts of the world, the "fight against terrorism" looks set to weaken not only the Islamic extremist groups that are its targets but also many NRMs. As minority religions that exist in tension within society, NRMs might well be victims of this seemingly unending "war." So what is the future for NRMs? NRM scholar Philip Charles Lucas has looked at the "ratcheting up of the international 'war on terror'" as well as at other factors that have previously been discussed in this book, including incidences of NRM violence and the "internationalization of the anticult and countercult movement." He has also remarked on the "efforts of traditional, 'national' churches to regain cultural hegemony by colluding with nationalist political forces" (for example, the way in which the Russian government and Orthodox Church have combined forces to curtail the growth of what they consider to be dangerous foreign religions). Overall, Lucas feels that "each of these factors plays a significant role in the increasingly repressive climate for new and minority religions around the globe."[9]

While Lucas's conclusion that "the future for NRMs and minority religions is not bright" is persuasive, it is not inarguable.[10] Other scholars believe that the anti-religious measures enacted by countries such as France, Russia, and China will be eventually swept away by the tide of growing global religious liberty. Whatever the merits of either of these predictions, it seems a safe bet that NRMs themselves, despite or even because of any laws restricting their growth, will continue to appear and struggle for survival. If history teaches us anything, it is that religious innovation and combination are basic components of our human condition.

Notes

Chapter 1

1   Melton in James R. Lewis, ed., *The Oxford Handbook of New Religious Movements* (Oxford: Oxford University Press, 2004), pp. 26–27.

2   See Peter Berger, *The Sacred Canopy* (New York: Doubleday, 1967).

3   Rodney Stark and William Sims Bainbridge, *The Future of Religion: Secularization, Revival and Cult Formation* (Berkeley, CA: University of California Press, 1985).

4   Charles Y. Glock, "The Role of Deprivation in the Origin and Evolution of Religious Groups," in R. Lee and M. Marty, eds., *Religion and Social Conflict* (New York: Oxford University Press, 1964), pp. 24–36.

5   Robert Bellah, "New Religious Consciousness and the Crisis of Modernity," in R. Bellah and C. Glock, eds., *The New Religious Consciousness* (Berkeley, CA: University of California Press, 1976), pp. 333–52.

Chapter 2

1   Episode 5F23: "The Joy of Sect," originally broadcast February 8, 1998.

2   James Lewis, *Legitimating New Religions* (New Brunswick, NJ: Rutgers University Press, 2003), p. 168.

3   Jonathan Z. Smith, "Religion, Religions, Religious," in Mark C. Taylor, ed. *Critical Terms for Religious Studies* (Chicago: University of Chicago Press, 1998), pp. 269–84.

4   Stephen R. Bokenkamp, *Early Daoist Scriptures* (Berkeley, CA: University of California Press, 1997), p. 11.

5   Philip Jenkins, *Mystics and Messiahs: Cults and New Religions in American History* (New York: Oxford University Press, 2000), p. 30.

6   Ibid., p. 29.

7   Jeffrey K. Hadden, "The Brainwashing Controversy," The Religious Movements Homepage Project, University of Virginia, http://religiousmovements.lib.virginia.edu/cultsect/brainwashing.htm (accessed January 19, 2006).

8   Quoted on website of the Rick A. Ross Institute, www.rickross.com/mind_control.html (accessed January 19, 2006).

9   St. Irenaeus of Lyons, *Against the Heresies*, translated and annotated by Dominic J. Unger (New York: Paulist Press, 1992).

Chapter 3

1   Robert Ellwood and Harry Partin, *Religious and Spiritual Groups in Modern America* (Englewood Cliffs, NJ: Prentice Hall, 1988).

2   Charles S. Braden, *Spirits in Rebellion: The Rise and Development of New Thought* (Dallas: Southern Methodist University Press, 1980), p. 54.

3   Ella Wheeler Wilcox, "Words" (1902), quoted in Braden 1980, p. 358.

4   See James R. Lewis and J. Gordon Melton, eds., *Perspectives on the New Age* (Albany, NY: State University of New York Press, 1992), especially the article "How New is the New Age?" by Robert Ellwood.

Chapter 4

1   Roger Finke and Rodney Stark, *The Churching of America* (New Brunswick, NJ: Rutgers University Press, 1992), p. 198. (The authors

also show that the supposedly staid 1950s saw a large growth of new spiritual movements. For a book-length treatment of that argument see Robert S. Ellwood, *The Fifties Spiritual Marketplace: American Religion in a Decade of Conflict* [New Brunswick, NJ: Rutgers University Press, 1997]).

Chapter 5

1   Two standard works on the subject are Daniel Overmyer, *Folk Buddhist Religion: Dissenting Sects in Late Traditional China* (Cambridge, MA: Harvard University Press, 1976) and Susan Naquin, *Millenarian Rebellion in China: The Eight Trigrams Uprising of 1813* (New Haven, CT: Yale University Press, 1976).

2   David Palmer, "Body cultivation in contemporary China," in James Miller, ed., *Chinese Religions in Contemporary Societies* (Santa Barbara, CA, ABC-CLIO, 2006), p. 156.

3   Helen Hardacre, *Kurozumikyo and the New Religions of Japan* (Princeton, NJ: Princeton University Press, 1986).

4   This document can be found in Gary Kessler, *Shinto Ways of Being Religious* (New York: McGraw-Hill, 2005), pp. 42–44, as well as online at: http://www.bbc.co.uk/religion/religions/shinto/features/nationalism/nation_3.s html

Chapter 6

1   Joseph Kimbangu (Simon Kimbangu's son), quoted in Benjamin C. Ray, *African Religions*, 2nd edition (Upper Saddle River, NJ: Prentice Hall, 2000), p. 175.

Chapter 7

1   Mark Sedgwick, "Establishments and Sects in the Islamic World," in Philip Charles Lucas and Thomas Robbins,

eds., *New Religious Movements in the 21st Century: Legal, Political, and Social Challenges in Global Perspective* (New York: Routledge, 2004).

2   Sedgwick 2004, p. 301.

3   Fouad Hussein, *Al-Zarqawi: Al-Qaida's Second Generation* (n.p., n.d.), quoted on Spiegel Online website, http://service.spiegel.de/cache/international (accessed March 2, 2006).

Chapter 8

1   Hugh B. Urban, *Tantra: Sex, Secrecy, Politics, and Power in the Study of Religion* (Berkeley, CA: University of California Press, 2003).

2   Irving Hexham and Karla Poewe, *New Religions as Global Cultures: Making the Human Sacred* (Boulder, CO: Westview Press, 1997), p. 42.

3   James Beckford, "New Religious Movements and Globalization," in Lucas and Robbins 2004, p. 256.

4   Douglas E. Cowan, *Cyberhenge: Modern Pagans on the Internet* (New York: Routledge, 2005).

5   Beckford in Lucas and Robbins 2004, p. 260.

6   For a summary of this argument see Lorne Dawson, *Comprehending Cults: The Sociology of New Religious Movements* (Toronto: Oxford University Press, 1998), Chapter 5.

7   The best summary of the Waco tragedy from the perspective of religious studies is James D. Tabor and Eugene V. Gallagher, *Why Waco?: Cults and the Battle for Religious Freedom in America* (Berkeley, CA: University of California Press, 1995).

8   See Daniele Hervieu-Leger, "France's Obsession with the 'Sectarian Threat,'" in Lucas and Robbins 2004, pp. 57–58.

9   Philip Charles Lucas, "The Future of New and Minority Religions in the Twenty-First Century: Religious Freedom under Global Siege," in Lucas and Robbins 2004, pp. 342–43.

10 Ibid., p. 354.

Glossary

Adventism Belief in the imminent second coming of Jesus Christ, particularly associated with the ministry of William Miller in the 1830s.

Aleph A Japanese NRM which changed its name from Aum Shinrikyo.

Anabaptist Religious movements that represented the radical wing of the Protestant reformation in the sixteenth century, calling for adult baptism and a removal from worldly affairs.

Buddhism A world religion founded by the Buddha in the fifth century B.C.E., which teaches enlightenment through cessation of desires.

channeling The act of receiving information from a consciousness outside one's own body.

Charismatic Refers to Christian groups that emphasize the Holy Spirit and which operate within other denominations or non-denominationally.

Christian Science Religion founded by Mary Baker Eddy in the 1870s, which maintains that because matter is illusion, illness can be overcome by purely spiritual means.

Church of Jesus Christ of Latter-day Saints/LDS The official name of the Mormon church, a widespread religion that reinterprets Christianity and was founded by Joseph Smith.

coven A small group of witches or neo-pagans, or a meeting of that group.

Daoism The indigenous religion of China, which focuses on rituals and techniques of bodily and spiritual transformation.

Druidism A recreation of the Celtic religion of pre-Christian Britain, now part of the broader neopagan movement.

ecumenical Concerned with promoting the unity of Christian churches.

esoteric Refers to a wide variety of traditions that see matter and spirit as a continuum and often include a mystical component.

Family, The An NRM founded in 1968 out of the Jesus People movement, formerly known as the Children of God.

fundamentalism Advocating a literal interpretation of Scripture, a union of religion and politics, and a rejection of modernity.

guru A Sanskrit word meaning spiritual teacher.

Hare Krishna *see* ISKCON

heresy A belief that contradicts the teaching of a given religious establishment.

Hermeticism Another term for the occult or esoteric tradition, named after Hermes Trismegistus, a legendary second-century C.E. writer on magic and alchemy.

Hinduism The dominant religion of India, incorporating a wide variety of deities and practices.

"human potential" movement A set of values and practices popularized in the 1960s that emphasize personal development through spirituality and psychology.

Islamist Name given by Western scholars to a number of modern movements within Islam that stress its incompatibility with the West.

ISKCON International Society of Krishna Consciousness, a Hindu devotional movement brought to the West in 1965, more colloquially known as Hare Krishna.

Jehovah's Witnesses A millennialist group, founded in 1881 out of the Adventist tradition, which engages in worldwide missionary activity.

Jesus People A movement that combined evangelical Christianity with a countercultural "hippie" lifestyle and which began in the 1960s on the West Coast of the U.S.

Kurozumikyo The earliest Japanese NRM, based on Shinto.

LDS *see* Church of Jesus Christ of Latter-day Saints.

Manicheanism A religion founded in third-century C.E. Persia, which taught that the world was the site of a struggle between equal forces of good and evil.

messianic Expecting a savior to redeem the world.

millennial The belief in the coming of a future Utopian age, and the end of the present one.

monism The theory that all reality is a unified whole.

Moonies *see* Unification Church.

Mormon *see* Church of Jesus Christ of Latter-day Saints.

neo-Confucianism A revival of Confucian philosophy and spirituality which began in eleventh-century China.

Neopagan A modern reaffirmation of ancient, indigenous, nature-based religions.

New Age A loosely structured spiritual movement dating from the 1970s, and peaking in the 1980s, with roots in earlier esoteric traditions.

Occultism Another term for the Hermetic or esoteric tradition, named because the tradition is secret.

Pentecostal Christian churches that emphasize the workings of the Holy Spirit, including speaking in tongues and divine healing, and which trace their history back to an early twentieth-century revival.

Puritans A group of Protestants in the sixteenth and seventeenth centuries who dissented from the Anglican Church and sought religious freedom in America.

Quakers The informal name for the Society of Friends, a movement founded in seventeenth-century England that rejects formal ministry or creed.

Rastafarian A religion originating in Jamaica in the 1930s, which venerates the former emperor of Ethiopia and stresses black nationalism.

Reformed Relating to the Protestant

tradition, which traces its lineage to John Calvin.

Rosicrucianism Relating to any of several international organizations that teach esotericism and claim descent from ancient sources.

Sant Mat A lineage of gurus from North India.

Scientology A religion founded by L. Ron Hubbard in 1954, incorporating modern psychology.

Shiite A branch of Islam, which makes up around 15% of all Muslims.

Shinto The indigenous religion of Japan, which acknowledges the sacred quality of nature and the presence of spirits known as *kami.*

Sikhism A monotheistic religion that began in India in the sixteenth century.

Spiritism A religion based on Spiritualism and founded by Allen Kardec in nineteenth-century France.

Spiritualism A religion that began in 1848 and believes in contacting the spirits of the dead.

Sunni A branch of Islam, which makes up around 85% of all Muslims.

syncretistic The combining of religious beliefs and practices from different traditions into one system.

Tantra Practices within Hinduism or Buddhism that forge a direct connection with the divine, sometimes in opposition to social norms.

Theosophy A religion that began in 1875, incorporating Buddhist, Hindu, and esoteric beliefs.

Unification Church Religious movement founded by Rev. Sun Myung Moon in 1954, formally known as the Family Federation of World Peace and Unification, and colloquially known as the Moonies.

White Lotus Secret Buddhist millennialist organizations in China.

Wicca *see* witchcraft

witchcraft The exercise of magical powers; practiced in many modern forms, most notably Wicca.

yoga A Sanskrit word meaning discipline and referring to any of several techniques to unite the self to the divine.

Zen A form of Buddhism that emphasizes enlightenment through meditation.

Suggested Further Reading

Chapter 1: What Are New Religious Movements?

General introductions to the subject of NRMs; I have restricted this list to quite recent publications.

PETER B. CLARKE, ed., *Encyclopedia of New Religious Movements* (New York: Routledge, 2005)
A reference work with over three hundred entries and a global perspective.

DERECK DASCHKE and W. MICHAEL ASHCRAFT, eds., *New Religious Movements: A Documentary Reader* (New York: New York University Press, 2005)
A collection of primary sources from a variety of NRMs.

LORNE DAWSON, *Comprehending Cults: The Sociology of New Religious Movements* (Toronto: Oxford University Press, 1998)
A clear, concise and balanced introduction to NRMs from a sociological point of view.

LORNE DAWSON, ed., *Cults and New Religious Movements: A Reader* (Malden, MA: Blackwell Publishing, 2003)
A carefully selected anthology of previously published chapters and articles on thematic aspects of new religions.

IRVING HEXHAM and KARLA POEWE, *New Religions as Global Cultures: Making the Human Sacred* (Boulder, CO: Westview Press, 1997)
A rather idiosyncratic introduction to new religions yet one which pays attention to its global dimension.

JAMES R. LEWIS, ed., *The Oxford Handbook of New Religious Movements* (Oxford: Oxford University Press, 2004)

JAMES R. LEWIS and JESPER AAGAARD PETERSEN, eds., *Controversial New Religions* (Oxford: Oxford University Press, 2005)
Two new edited volumes with useful information on specific NRMs as well as topical issues.

J. GORDON MELTON, *Encyclopedia of American Religions*, 7th ed. (Detroit: Gale, 2003)
Addresses, phone numbers, and websites for virtually every religious group in the U.S., as well as helpful essays on each "religious family."

TIMOTHY MILLER, ed., *America's Alternative Religions* (Albany, NY: SUNY Press, 1995)
Short chapters on the most important NRMs in the U.S.

CHRISTOPHER PARTRIDGE, ed., *New Religions: A Guide* (New York: Oxford University Press, 2004)
An illustrated encyclopedia of NRMs, with a global scope.

JOHN A. SALIBA, *Understanding New Religious Movements*, 2nd ed. (Walnut Creek, CA: AltaMira Press, 2003)
Separate chapters on sociological, psychological, and theological dimensions of NRMs.

STEPHEN STEIN, *Communities of Dissent: Alternative Religions in America* (New York: Oxford University Press, 2003)
Although written for a high school audience, this is a masterful historical synthesis.

Chapter 2: NRMs as Modern Heresy

DAVID CHRISTIE-MURRAY, *A History of Heresy* (London: New English Library, 1976)
A standard work on heresy.

JOHN B. HENDERSON, *The Construction of Orthodoxy and Heresy: Neo-Confucian, Islamic, Jewish and early

Christian patterns (Albany, NY: SUNY Press, 1998)
Quite technical in parts but useful in showing how heresy is a basic category of religious thought.

PHILIP JENKINS, *Mystics and Messiahs: Cults and New Religions in American History* (New York: Oxford University Press, 2000)
A very readable history of cult scares of the last 150 years.

JAMES LEWIS, *Legitimating New Religions* (New Brunswick, NJ: Rutgers University Press, 2003)
While the first half describes how NRMs legitimate themselves through the use of science, history, etc., the second half is about how NRMs have been delegitimated by the media and other parties.

Chapter 3: NRMs as Esoteric Revival

MICHAEL F. BROWN, *The Channeling Zone* (Cambridge, MA: Harvard Press, 1997)
An anthropological treatment of channels and channeling groups, both large and small.

BRUCE CAMPBELL, *Ancient Wisdom Revived: A History of the Theosophical Movement* (Berkeley, CA: University of California Press, 1980)
A sympathetic and readable history of Theosophy and its offshoots.

TOBIAS CHURTON, *Gnostic Philosophy: From Ancient Persia to Modern Times* (Rutland, VT: Inner Traditions, 2005)
A helpful introduction, though not particularly scholarly.

ROBERT ELLWOOD and HARRY PARTIN, *Religious and Spiritual Groups in Modern America* (Englewood Cliffs, NJ: Prentice Hall 1988)
Contains a lengthy chapter that argues that many current NRMs are esoteric revival movements.

ANTOINE FAIVRE and JACOB NEEDLEMAN, eds., *Modern Esoteric Spirituality* (New York: Crossroad, 1992)
Groundbreaking essays that define and chart esotericism from the Renaissance to the present day.

WOUTER HANEGRAAFF, *New Age Religion and Western Culture* (Albany, NY: SUNY Press, 1996)
A comprehensive intellectual history of the New Age movement.

JAMES R. LEWIS, *The Encyclopedic Sourcebook of New Age Religions* (Amherst, NY: Prometheus Books, 2004)
An odd but useful assortment of primary sources plus informational and theoretical essays on everything from channeling to Theosophy.

CHRISTOPHER PARTRIDGE, ed., *UFO Religions* (New York and London: Routledge, 2003)
Useful studies of specific UFO NRMs, often pointing out their Theosophical origins.

D. MICHAEL QUINN, *Early Mormonism and the Magic World View* (Salt Lake City, UT: Signature Books, 1987)
An important book detailing the esoteric origins of Mormonism.

Chapter 4: NRMs as Asian Missions to the West

RICK FIELDS, *How the Swans Came to the Lake: A Narrative History of Buddhism in America* (Boston: Shambhala Press, 1986)
A classic account by a Buddhist journalist.

KEN RAWLINSON, *The Book of Enlightened Masters* (Chicago: Open Court Press, 1997)
A fascinating guide to Hindu, Buddhist, and Sufi teachers and their lineages active in the West.

RICHARD SEAGER, *Buddhism in America* (New York: Columbia University Press: 1999)
A beautifully written introduction.

RICHARD HUGHES SEAGER, *Encountering the Dharma: Daisaku Ikeda, Soka Gakkai, and the Globalization of Buddhist Humanism* (Berkeley, CA: University of California Press, 2006)

THOMAS TWEED and STEPHEN PROTHERO, *Asian Religions in America: A Documentary History* (New York: Oxford University Press, 1999)
A selection of wonderful primary sources, each with a helpful introduction.

Chapter 5: New Religions in East Asia

MARIA H. CHANG, *Falun Gong: The End of Days* (New Haven, CT: Yale University Press, 2004)
A discussion of Falun gong's beliefs and practices as well as the Chinese government's case against the NRM.

PETER B. CLARKE, ed., *Japanese New Religions in Global Perspective* (Richmond, Surrey: Curzon Press, 2000)
Essays about Japanese NRMs in Brazil, Europe, etc.

HELEN HARDACRE, *Kurozumikyo and the New Religions of Japan* (Princeton, NJ: Princeton University Press, 1986)
An important work that provides insight into the worldview of Japanese NRMs.

H. NEILL MCFARLAND, *The Rush Hour of the Gods: A Study of New Religious Movements in Japan* (New York: Macmillan, 1967)
Out of date, but readable and a classic in NRM literature.

DAVID PALMER, *Qigong Fever: Body, Science and the Poltics of Religion in China, 1949–1999* (London: Hurst, forthcoming)
The first comprehensive history of qigong groups in mainland China.

B.J. TER HAAR, *The White Lotus Teachings in Chinese Religious History* (Honolulu: University of Hawaii Press, 1999)
An up-to-date work on the White Lotus groups.

Chapter 6: New Religions of Africa and the African Diaspora

PHILIP JENKINS, *The Next Christendom* (New York: Oxford University Press, 2002)
A few chapters have good summaries of the rise of new forms of Christianity in Africa.

BENNETTA JULES-ROSETTE, ed., *The New Religions of Africa* (Norwood, NJ: Ablex Publishing, 1979)
A classic collection of studies of African NRMs, both Christian and not. Still one of the only books of its kind.

JOSEPH MURPHY, *Working the Spirit: Ceremonies of the African Diaspora* (Boston: Beacon Press, 1994)
A very readable book on Santeria, Vodou, Rastafarianism, and other NRMs.

Chapter 7: Islamic New Religions

JASON BURKE, *Al-Qaeda: The True Story of Radical Islam* (London: Penguin, 2004)
A recent addition to the growing library on Al-Qaeda; this one pays particular attention to its religious dimension.

WILLIAM C. CHITTICK, *Sufism: A Short Introduction* (Oxford: Oneworld Publications, 2000)
A readable and sympathetic guide.

MICHAEL MCMULLEN, *The Baha'i: The Religious Construction of a Global Identity* (New Brunswick, NJ: Rutgers University Press, 2000)
A case study of the Baha'i community of Atlanta, Georgia and one of the few full-length academic works on this NRM.

Chapter 8: The Global Future of New Religious Movements

DAVID BROMLEY and J. GORDON MELTON, eds., *Cults, Religion, and Violence* (Cambridge: Cambridge University Press, 2002)
Separate essays on every major episode of NRM-related violence to date, plus theoretical considerations.

LORNE DAWSON and DOUGLAS E. COWAN, eds., *Religion Online: Finding Faith on the Internet* (New York: Routledge, 2004)
A few chapters deal specifically with NRMs online.

PHILIP CHARLES LUCAS and THOMAS ROBBINS, eds., *New Religious Movements in the 21st Century: Legal, Political, and Social Challenges in Global Perspective* (New York: Routledge, 2004)
With essays about NRMs in all regions of the world, this is essential reading.

Websites

1. **A selected list of recommended, academically neutral websites on NRMs.**

Religious Movements Homepage at the University of Virginia:
http://religiousmovements.lib.virginia.edu

Gene Thursby's New Religions Site:
http://www.religiousworlds.com/newreligions.html

Hartford Institute for Religion Research:
http://hirr.hartsem.edu/org/faith_new_religious_movements.html

Cesnur: Center for Studies on New Religions:
http://www.cesnur.org

Online texts about cults and new religions:
http://www.skepsis.nl/onlinetexts.html

Ontario Consultants on Religious Tolerance:
http://www.religioustolerance.org/nurel.htm

2. **Websites of NRMs (and a few of their opponents) in the order they are mentioned in the text.**

Chapter 1: What Are New Religious Movements?

New Age spirituality in Glastonbury
http://www.glastonbury.co.uk/spirituality/index.htm
http://www.glastonburytor.org.uk

Aum Shinrikyo
http://english.aleph.to/

Church of Jesus Christ of the Latter-day Saints
http://lds.org

Chapter 2: NRMs as Modern Heresy

Mennonite Church U.S.A.
http://www.mennoniteusa.org

Catholic Refutation of the Maria Monk Story
http://www.catholicleague.org/research/mariamonk.htm

Christian Research Institute, a countercult movement
http://www.equip.org

Rick Ross Institute, a well-known deprogrammer
http://www.rickross.com

American Family Foundation (an anticult movement now called The International Cultic Studies Association)
http://www.csj.org

The Unification Church
http://www.unification.org

Chapter 3: NRMs as Esoteric Revival

Gnostic Society (a modern Gnostic church based in Los Angeles with a very informative website) http://www.gnosis.org

General Church of the New Jerusalem (a small Christian denomination based on the writings of Emanuel Swedenborg)
http://www.newchurch.org

National Spiritualist Association of Churches
http://www.nsac.org

Theosophical Society (Adyar)
http://www.theosophical.org

Christian Science
http://www.tfccs.org

International New Thought Alliance
http://www.newthoughtalliance.org

Unity Churches
www.unity.org

Church Universal and Triumphant
http://www.tsl.org

Hermetic Order of the Golden Dawn (one
of several contemporary groups that uses
the name)
http://www.hermeticgoldendawn.org

Heaven's Gate
http://www.heavensgate.com

The Raelians
http://rael.org

Aetherius Society
http://www.aetherius.org

Scientology
http://www.scientology.org

Lazaris
http://www.lazaris.com

Ramtha
http://www.ramtha.com

Pagans (There are many, many Pagan
websites. Here are some important and
helpful ones):
The Pagan Federation (a long-established
British umbrella group)
http://www.paganfed.org

Covenant of the Goddess (an American
umbrella group)
http://www.cog.org

Church of All Worlds (one of the first
recognized American Pagan groups)
http://www.caw.org

The Covenant of Unitarian Universalist
Pagans
http://www.cuups.org

Chapter 4: NRMs as Asian Missions to the West

The Brahmo Samaj
http://www.thebrahmosamaj.org

Arya Samaj (this is the American branch)
http://www.aryasamaj.com

Ramakrishna Movement
http://www.sriramakrishna.org

Vedanta Society (this is the Southern
California branch, which has the most

comprehensive website)
http://www.vedanta.org

Self Realization Fellowship
http://www.yogananda-srf.org

San Francisco Zen Center
http://www.sfzc.org

Friends of the Western Buddhist Order
http://www.fwbo.org

Chogyam Trungpa
http://www.shambhala.org

Transcendental Meditation
http://www.tm.org

Integral Yoga
http://www.yogaville.org

Siddha Yoga
http://www.siddhayoga.org

ISKCON
http://www.iskcon.com

Sikh Dharma (3HO)
http://www.3ho.org

Élan Vital (Divine Light Mission)
http://www.elanvital.org

Eckankar
http://www.eckankar.org

Soka Gakkai International
www.sgi.org

Chapter 5: New Religions in East Asia

Yiguandao (world I-kuan-Tao
headquarters, based in Los Angeles)
http://www.with.org

True Jesus Church
http://www.tjc.org

The Local Church (i.e. The Shouters)
www.localchurches.org

Yan Xin qigong
http://www.yanxinqigong.net

Falun gong
http://www.falundafa.org

Cao Dai (there is no official website but
this one represents a group of missionaries
abroad)
http://www.caodai.net

Cheondogyo (in Korean)
http://www.chondogyo.or.kr

Jeungsando
http://www.jeungsando.org

DahnHak
http://www.healingsociety.org

Kurozumikyo
http://www.kurozumikyo.com

Tenrikyo
http://www.tenrikyo.or.jp

Konkokyo
http://www.konkokyo.or.jp/eng

Reiyukai
http://www.reiyukai.org

Rissho Kosei-kai
http://www.rk-world.org

Perfect Liberty Kyodan (This helpful
English language site is from the
Canadian branch)
http://www.perfectliberty.ca

Makuya
http://www.makuya.or.jp/eng

Mahikari
http://www.mahikari.org

Chapter 6: New Religions of Africa and the African Diaspora

Few African churches (the Kimbanguist
Church included) have their own websites.
The Nazareth Baptist Church is best
represented on this webpage from a
Canadian scholar of African new
religions:

http://www.acs.ucalgary.ca/~nurelweb/book
s/shembe/s-index.html

Church of the Lord (Aladura) (One of the
largest Nigerian Aladura Churches)
http://www.aladura.de

Deeper Life Bible Church
http://www.dclm.org

Vodou. Obviously there is no central site
for Vodou. Most of the plentiful "voodoo"
sites come out of the New Orleans
tradition. This Vodou temple in North
America seems to have a genuine
connection with an institution in Haiti:
http://www.vodou.org

Santeria Church of the Lukumi Babalu Aye
http://www.church-of-the-lukumi.org

Universal Negro Improvement Association
http://www.unia-acl.org

Nation of Islam (Farrakhan)
http://www.noi.org

Chapter 7: Islamic New Religions

Islam has no official organization, and thus
no official website. Here is the best overall
site for learning about aspects of Islam,
including the topics discussed in this
chapter:

Resources for Studying Islam
http://www.arches.uga.edu/~godlas

Ahmadiyya Muslims
http://www.alislam.org

Sufi Order International
http://www.sufiorder.org

Haqqani Naqshbandi Sufi Order
http://www.naqshbandi.org

Meher Baba (There is no single Meher
Baba organization. The British Meher Baba
association is a good place to start)
http://www.meherbaba.co.uk

Most "fundamentalist Islamic"
organizations have no official websites in
English. One that does is Jamaat-e-Islami
http://www.jamaat.org

Baha'i
http://bahai.org

"Orthodox" Baha'i
http://www.tarbiyacenter.org

Chapter 8: The Global Future of New Religious Movements

Osho
http://www.osho.com

Western Reform Taoism
http://www.wrt.org

Church of Moo
http://www.churchofmoo.com

NOTE: Web addresses are not stable. These
URLs were current as of March 1, 2006.

Index